2009 — B...

D0329678

Go,

Go, Tell Michelle

African American Women Write to the New First Lady

Compiled and edited by

and Barbara A. Seals Nevergold

Peggy Brooks-Bertram

ee

EXCELSIOR EDITIONS

STATE UNIVERSITY OF NEW YORK PRESS

ALBANY, NEW YORK

Published by State University of New York Press, Albany

© 2009 State University of New York

All rights reserved

Printed in the United States of America

For information, contact
State University of New York Press, Albany, NY
www.sunypress.edu

Production by Ryan Morris
Marketing by Fran Keneston

Library of Congress Cataloging-in-Publication Data
Go, tell Michelle : African American women write to the new First Lady /
compiled and edited by Barbara A. Seals Nevergold and Peggy Brooks-Bertram.
    p. cm.
  ISBN 978-1-4384-2918-2   (pbk. : alk. paper)
    1. African American women.   2. Obama, Michelle, 1964–   3. Presidents'
spouses—United States—Correspondence.   I. Nevergold, Barbara Seals.
II. Brooks-Bertram, Peggy, 1943–
  E185.86.G58 2009
  973.932092—dc22   2008053693

10   9   8   7   6   5   4   3   2

Contents

Foreword

This extraordinary collection of letters to Michelle Obama says a great deal about the lives, the hopes, prayers, fears, and aspirations of African American women today. Letters sent to any famous person from total strangers ultimately say more about the writers than about the recipient. In these letters we read a great deal of autobiography, as the writers seek to share their stories with the woman who will soon be First Lady of the United States of America. Evoking tales of our ancestors is an ancient tradition in many African cultures, and a tradition very familiar to African Americans. We gauge our progress and our survival against our memory of the generations that have come before us.

Interestingly, the first letter written to President-elect Barack Obama, of which I was aware, was the open letter from Alice Walker, and her message was largely about his wife, Michelle. The celebrated African American novelist urged the President-elect to remember that he "did not create the disaster that the world is experiencing, and that he alone is not responsible for bringing the world back to balance." She reminded him, instead, that:

a primary responsibility that you do have . . . is to cultivate happiness in your own life. To make a schedule that permits sufficient time of rest and play with your gorgeous wife and lovely daughters.

Like so many other African American women, Alice Walker is concerned for the personal life of the new President and our new First Lady. This is understandable, for Michelle Obama's life has become the realization of dreams we have for all African American women—success, respect, power over our destiny, and the ability to exert a positive influence on the nation and the world.

"First Lady" is not an elected position, is not an official title, bears no official responsibilities, and earns no salary. Still, the job does come with a hefty roster of expectations. In that regard, we learn a great deal from letters to previous first ladies. For example, it used to be a tradition at the White House for the First Lady to invite congressional wives to an annual tea. In 1929, one of those wives was Lou DePriest, the African American wife of Representative Oscar DePriest of Illinois, the twentieth century's first African American congressman. Mrs. Herbert Hoover received the following letter from a nameless spokesperson for the Women's League of Miami, viciously condemning her for extending the invitation:

Dear Mrs. H. Hoover,
We thought we were putting a "real" White "Lady" in the White House. Didn't even dream that you would disgrace the White House by associating with Negroes. . . . You can go to Illinois next winter and visit your Negro friend. FLORIDA don't care for you to visit the South anymore.

Well, now an African American lady from *Illinois* is headed to the White House for a prolonged stay, after her husband won the state of *Florida*. During her time in the White House, the sorts of letters Michelle Obama receives will change. Some will make demands of her, or beg favors from her; others will criticize or praise her. For now, however, as the first African American First Lady, Michelle Obama would seem to fulfill a unique set of dreams and aspirations, even as she provokes new dreams, aspirations—and dare we mention, fears. In this collection, there are letters that echo those once written to Mrs. Kennedy and to Mrs. Lincoln urging Mrs. Obama to be "safe," or reminding her that she is "in our prayers," or that she needs to "protect" her husband.

Though women—and men—from a diverse range of backgrounds certainly can identify with her, or with any first lady—(Queen Victoria of England famously wrote a heart-wrenching letter of condolence to the widow of the author of the Emancipation Proclamation, Mary Todd Lincoln)—Michelle Obama obviously holds a special meaning for African American women. We seem to recognize her as one of our own. We are simultaneously proud of her, seek to protect her, and to encourage her. And our expectations for her are obviously very high. She has not even moved into the White House, and already we hear that she is to be an Eleanor Roosevelt for our times, and by implication, for our people.

The women who have written letters in this collection are highly accomplished and hail from a broad spectrum of backgrounds. So, too, is the recipient. Born in 1964, Michelle LaVaughn Robinson Obama is a graduate of Princeton University and of Harvard Law School; she met Barak Obama when they were both employed at the same law firm and she was assigned to mentor him. We have only just begun to know this complex young woman, and we are never likely to know her fully.

American First Ladies are, instantaneously and inevitably, among the most famous people in the world, but as we learn from First Ladies of the past—from Eleanor Roosevelt, to Jackie Kennedy, to Pat Nixon—though familiar to us, these women are ultimately enigmatic. Nonetheless, they help us know ourselves better. Through Mrs. Roosevelt we gauge our own devotion to social justice and international harmony. Jacqueline Kennedy, like Coretta Scott King, became the measure of our own dignity in grief. Hillary Rodham Clinton fulfilled the feminist ideal that a woman need not live in her husband's shadow—even if that husband is the President of the United States.

So far, Michelle Obama is serving to help us see ourselves at our best. We see validation of our choices and our values. Even the decision to have her mother accompany the family to the White House resonates with many African American women who have lived in three-generation homes; when Michelle is obliged to remain at a state dinner until late at night, Grandma will be on hand to fulfill the family bedtime ritual. So many of us know the burdens of having a working mother—albeit, not a mother with such high-profile responsibilities. In Michelle Obama, we see reflected the face of hope; the face of inclusion; the face of America as the proverbial land of opportunity, equality, and justice.

Like the other African American women who have written in this volume, I too wish her great happiness in the White House. I wish her great success in the attainment of her goals for her husband and daughters, and for the causes that are dear to her. I too hope that wonderful things will happen for our nation and for the world while the Obama family is in residence at 1600 Pennsylvania Avenue. This moment has been a long time in coming.

Muriel A. Howard, PhD
President
Buffalo State College
Buffalo, New York

Preface

Choosing a title for any book is serious business. The original title for this book was *Dear Michelle: Messages of Encouragement, Support and Love to the New First Lady*. For the better part of three weeks, we operated with this title, and all of the letters and poems we received were under this title. When we sent a draft document to the publisher with that title, the publisher responded quickly saying, "How about 'Go Tell Michelle.' It's more dynamic and has more action. Sleep on it and tell me what you think." We slept on it and agreed. However, we made a major change, we added a simple punctuation device, a comma. Now we not only had dynamics, we had specific action: [You go] and [you tell] Michelle. From no comma to comma the title now issued a specific directive as well as a recipient of the action: [You] go and write a letter or poem and tell [Who?], Michelle.

The comma established a historic and appropriate voice and took us back to the title of an old Negro spiritual sung by America's enslaved and probably Michelle's great-great-grandparents on the Friendfield Plantation in Georgetown, South Carolina. The Negro spiritual is "Go, Tell It on the Mountain." Most, if not all of us never noticed the comma separating *go* from *tell*, creating two distinct actions invoking both movement and voice. Presumably created first in the early 1800s by slaves, it was first popularized in 1879 when performed by the Jubilee Singers of Fisk University. In 1907, John W. Work, a musicologist and lover of Negro spirituals, wrote the melody and music and included it in his book of Negro spirituals. Written in irregular meter with a Negro melody, in G Major, Black folks are directed to "Go" and shout the good news from the mountain top and tell [it]; that a momentous and nearly unimaginable event had occurred.

We are not sure when and how the comma was introduced into the title, but no doubt, Work understood the power of this device, and the comma remained in his 1907 version, more than a hundred years past the first naming of the spiritual. We understood it as well. Judging from the words of the hundreds of contributors submitting letters and poems to this book, only one hundred of which are represented here, they, too, understood. The strategy of invoking voice and movement is a call and response staple in the sermons of the Black church. We are reminded of the words of Black ministers in Sunday morning service when in religious and fervent passion, they shout to their congregations, "Now go tell that . . . ," a direct connection to the old spiritual, "Go, Tell It on the Mountain."

In *Go, Tell Michelle* we asked African American women around the country and the world to "tell [it]," their prayers, heartfelt words of encouragement, support, and love to Michelle. In their profound exuberance they encouraged others to "tell [it]," and spread the word. Many responded.

In this age of digital technology with a personal message merely an email away, these women engaged others in telling it. In telling it, from the West Coast to the East Coast and across the Atlantic, they shared sentiments from their mountain tops, their hills, and their valleys. They announced it, their personal feelings about the momentous and spectacular occasion of the ascendancy of President-elect Obama and his soul mate, Michelle Obama, to the highest political mountain in the world. We are both humbled and honored to share with readers only a few of the many letters and poems of women of color who joined us in telling it to Michelle, the first African American First Lady in the history of the United States of America. We are confident Michelle will see and hear it in these poems and letters.

Acknowledgments

No major endeavor of this sort, executed in a very short time frame, can be successfully completed without the support of many people and organizations. In this regard, we are indebted to President John B. Simpson, University at Buffalo; Thomas Slomka, Director of Projects at the University at Buffalo, Digital Libraries; Stacy Person, Director of Collections, University at Buffalo, Digital Libraries; Stephanie Kreutter, Student Assistant, University at Buffalo; W. David Penniman, Executive Director, Nylink, who encouraged us and introduced us to executives at State University of New York Press; to Carole Petro and the staff of WBFO Radio at University at Buffalo who conducted our first interview on the book and then paved the way for an interview with National Public Radio. We are indebted to the African American and African women around the world who responded to our call for their letters and poems. We also acknowledge the women of all races who understood exactly what we were trying to do and added their voices of support.

Finally, we thank our families, our husbands, and our children for their unwavering support and encouragement.

This book is dedicated to our mothers, Margaret Gilliam Brooks and Clara Ellis Seals.

Introduction

If we had any doubt that Barack Obama was the best candidate for the presidency of the United States, those reservations disappeared on January 3 when he won the Iowa caucus. Obama declared the win a "defining moment in history" and a clear signal that the American people agreed with his message of change. The Iowa caucus victory and its impact on the course of the Obama campaign also raised the visibility of Michelle Obama. For the first time, we were struck by the realization that if Barack Obama made history as the first African American President, his wife would become the first African American First Lady. The prospect of these two historic "firsts" was exhilarating. We joined millions, African Americans and other people of color, who began to believe that the impossible, a Black President in our lifetime, was possible.

Throughout the months after Iowa, like so many other Americans, we were increasingly engrossed in the day-to-day campaign news and emotionally vested in its outcome. We followed the course of the controversies that threatened to derail the campaign and applauded our new President-elect for his disciplined, calm, and steady response to each new attempt to end his quest for the presidency. And at the same time we developed a new respect and admiration for Michelle. She was becoming an increasingly visible and vocal presence at her husband's side, backing him or representing him as she spoke to audiences around the country. Through the worst of times and the best of times, she appeared to be an equal partner with her husband and matched him in style and substance. In his own words, Obama described Michelle as his "best friend, love of my life and rock of our family."

We got to know her better during the Democratic National Convention. "Each of us comes here tonight by way of our improbable journey." With these words, Michelle Obama began her speech on the eve of her husband's historic nomination as the party's candidate for President of the United States. As she continued, she described herself by the roles she considered essential elements that define who she is: a sister, wife, mother, and daughter. Her moving presentation left no doubt as to what she valued and confirmed our growing esteem and sense of solidarity with this woman.

When Michelle became the target of media misrepresentation and stereotyping, we saw her strength and resilience. We were incensed when she was accused of being un-American because of remarks, taken out of context, about being "really proud" of her country for the first time in her life. But *The New Yorker* magazine cover that depicted her as a gun-toting, terrorist, angry Black woman was the final straw! Black women, everywhere, felt the sting of indignation, decried this caricature and rushed to embrace and defend this beautiful, graceful, intelligent woman. We commended her ability to rise above the derision and distraction. On November 4, we greeted the historic election of Barack Hussein Obama with joy, excitement, hope, and optimism. Our feelings of love and sisterhood with Michelle, our future First Lady, were intertwined in the onslaught of our other emotions.

We have provided this backdrop because we believe that the idea for this book was planted during that "defining historic moment" when Barack Obama won the Iowa caucus. It was watered, fertilized, and took root at various times during the long campaign as we became intimately and resolutely committed to the Obama campaign and its principal leaders, Barack and Michelle. We had long conversations about our belief that as an African American woman, our new first lady will have greater expectations and more rigorous demands placed upon her than previous first ladies. Further, in the back of our minds, usually unspoken but ever present, we have a heightened concern about the safety of the Obama family as they undertake this new position as the first family of this nation. A few days after the election on an unusually mild, sunny day in western New York, one of us said, "I have an idea" and the leaves and stems of a new seedling pushed through the earth!

The call for papers for a publication was sent out on November 11, a week after the election. We asked women to send us letters and creative writings to share with our incoming First Lady, noting that "as African American women, we want to send her a special message, grounded in our common ancestry and in the belief that our daughters have not only been inspired by her accomplishments but empowered by her example." The call went out through the Uncrowned Queens List-serve and on our website. It was picked up by other websites and list-serves, but one of the most dynamic methods for getting the word out was old-fashioned word-of-mouth. Given a brief time frame, inclusive of the Thanksgiving holiday, the call was very effective. We received over one hundred and fifty submissions in the three-week period. In fact, at this writing, we are still receiving calls and email with letters attached from women who are anxious to have their messages included in this publication.

How did they respond? These authors saw the call for letters as their chance to connect with one of their own and hoped that a personal letter or poem might be handed personally to the First Lady. Their writings are awesome. As if dressed for a celebration, their words danced on the page in scripts of elegance and style befitting a First Lady: Chicago, CAC Champagne, Lucinda Handwriting, Edwardian Script ITC, Rage Italic, and Onyx. The publisher requires Courier, in a 12-point font size. They wrote prayer-filled letters with solemn remembrances of distant and close ancestors. Their letters beautifully document the African American past on these shores. They tied themselves, Michelle, and all of us, to the African continent with solemn remembrance of the Middle Passage. They crafted breathtaking poetry like "Helium Hopes": "You are my balloon tickling the feet of God, Favor filled, Celestially covered, And tied to my string, Is pride." Sarmiento's words shout from the page: "We hollered, we all screamed . . . shouted Hallelujah, . . . we sisters celebrated you MICHELLE OBAMA," and from Amira Davis: "You are there because our mothers prayed."

Who were these women? This is an era of digital danger with spam, phishing, identify theft, and high possibility of online crimes. There is endless but legitimate caution about strangers soliciting information online. We wondered about the public reaction to our request for letters. We asked ourselves: Who would respond to such a call for letters? Who would write to total strangers during the Thanksgiving holiday and even on the day itself? Who would send letters and poems from Blackberries while being driven to grandmother's house for Thanksgiving dinner? Who would bare their souls in letters they only hoped could be read by First Lady Obama? Who would send emails around the world encouraging "Sistahs" to join them in writing a letter to the wife of Number 44? Realizing the importance of the moment for women of color, White women, many strong supporters of both Barack and Michelle, called their Black "Sistahs" and their Black daughter-in-laws and urged them to respond.

Women with ancestry from the broad African diaspora responded, including countries in Africa, the islands of Jamaica and Puerto Rico, African Americans and First Nation's women across the United States. In brief biographies, respondents described themselves as hair dressers, office workers, retirees, leaders in Black women's organizations, tenured professors, university presidents, health care professionals, evangelists, business women, and senior citizens. Some described themselves as "just a simple person" needing to write to Michelle. From young mothers to octogenarians the letters came, all singing the praises of Michelle Obama. And, then, there were the poets, some poet laureates, whose early morning Muses dictated lyrical poems bringing tears with each reading like Arlette Miller Smith: "In anticipation of you coming from the south & side and shoulders of the sisterhood, We sing, pray . . . raise and lift you up for such a time as this."

Who did they speak for? These authors spoke in many voices as well as their own. They spoke for children lost prematurely, for their living and lost mothers, grandmothers, and great-grandmothers. They spoke for their husbands. They spoke for children not yet in the womb but who could be welcomed now that Michelle was in what Mercier described as Rainbow House: "Never wanted to visit the White House till now . . . now that you and your family live there by proclamation of rainbow vote and universal prayer." In each letter, authors spoke of the presence of the spirit of our African ancestors. They called the names of former slaves from their families and the names of African American freedom fighters on whose shoulders we all stand like Fannie Lou Hamer, Nannie Helen Burroughs, and Ida B. Wells. Others remembered women of African antiquity like Queen Hatshepsut and others. Still others expressed reverence for the Black souls and spirits whose bodies had been in chains in the Middle Passage and the Mississippi Delta but whose spirits are "dancing all around Heaven," in celebration of Michelle.

What did we accomplish? For the past decade, the primary work of the Uncrowned Queens Institute for Research and Education, Incorporated, has been to help African American women find their voice in saluting themselves, their friends, and community. Through the institute's web page at www. uncrownedqueens.com, we invited them to tell their stories in their own words and we published their self-written biographies and their photographs online. This book is a continuation of that work. We are committed to maintaining a historic archive on how African American women viewed and documented this occasion for themselves and others.

WE IN ANTICIPATION OF YOU
For Michelle Obama, First Lady/Mother & the First Family

WE

> Vomited, swallowed & engorged oceanic passages
> sardined inside the darkness of carriers that moved
> culture, kindred, and home from tribal remembrance
> to enslaved reality.

WE

> Unlocked new world / words & hid learning
> seldom to be uttered aloud or mistaken as
> schooled vessels bright, deep, & full of knowing.

WE

> Spread legs heavy with nonchalance frozen within
> rhythmic thrusts pounding captive life inside walls of
> wailing water.

WE

> Baked sun and resolve muscled under barren shares
> cropped
> without buds & blossoms chopped & hoed from
> unyielding dusty ground.

WE

> Housed, cooked, & clean scrubbed Mizz Ann's rolled
> & pinned/t up orders
> inside crisp collared rooms fragrant with simmering
> rage and stirring silence.

WE

Clubbed colored women's character assassinated by
jacked up news white
With assumed high-natured hotness loosed on
supposedly innocent men
Waiting to be aroused.

WE

Countered lunch with colored water washed down in
jailed service
around back doors, buses & balconies in picture show
black and whiteness.

WE

Booked Black dreams in ivory towers teetering in terror
as shaken foundations, hallowed halls, & ivied walls
braced & braved the new world, collegially colored
with promise.
In anticipation of your coming from the south & side
and shoulders of the sisterhood,

WE

sing,
    pray,
        shout,
            teach,
                preach,
                    raise & lift
                    you up for such a time as this.

WE

admire the brilliant light of First Lady torches passed on
to you:
Eleanor Roosevelt's long arm of justice & consciousness
extended with voice & conviction to the discriminated,
dismissed, & discharged whether soldier, worker or a
gifted singer whose silenced song died in the throats of
unrevolutionary American daughters.

Jackie Kennedy's elegant young grace punctuated with
beauty, art, & culture enshrined through time within
rooms restored in a nation's house.
Hillary Rodham Clinton's herstoric climb from an
Arkansas mansion to the house on a hill of hope to a
seat for stately senators to a country race though lost
wins & begins a different free world post . . .
But WE will never forget the watery & windy journeys
that gave rise to y/our *1–20–09 1600 new birth of
freedom so*

WE — in anticipation of you —

RODE thru
the middle passage; colonized bodies but renewed
spirit; lynching and lost of brothers brave and
sisters strong; segregated south/side and polarized
north end; stinging water hoses and cracking clubs;
villains & victims of violence; & the hatred that
hinders our hope.

WE

Armed & armored you & y/ours with the wisdom,
wherewithal, and [mother] wit of foremother/ activists
who — were/are not God — but who, in anticipation
of you, knew that this time would surely come and all
we carried, dreamed, hoped, dared and desired would,
at last, be lifted & delivered from
the shoulders of Sojourner Truth;
the soapbox of Maria Stewart;
the feet of Harriet Tubman;
the words of Phyllis Wheatley, Frances Harper &
Anna Julia Cooper;
the song of Marian Anderson;
the church woman's education of Nannie
Helen Burroughs;
the court & news rooms of Mary Ann Shadd Cary;

the sacrifice & service of Anna Murray Douglass;
the spiritual awakening of Jarena Lee, Amanda
  Berry Smith & Julia Foote —
all armed, armored & amazing foremother/
  ancestors in anticipation of you . . .

Arlette Miller Smith

Arlette Miller Smith is an Associate Professor in the Department of English and codirector of the African American Studies minor at St. John Fisher College in Rochester, New York. Arlette is a Black Literary Herstorian who chronicles the herstory of her African American people and their armored resistance to oppression, discrimination, and invisibility.

Dear Michelle,

My wonderful Aunt Lillie passed away a few years ago. She had lived for a century. Her grandfather had been a slave on the Burnt Quarter Plantation in Virginia. For more than forty years, she worked at a bakery in the Miller and Rhoades Department Store in Richmond, Virginia. When I was a child, she made many visits to my home in Baltimore, Maryland. Whenever my family fell on hard times—and it was often—my mother would send for Aunt Lillie. She would always come. We would meet her at the Greyhound Bus Station. She never traveled light. She had several plaid suitcases with leather buckles tied together with assorted straps to secure the contents. Filled to bursting, the suitcases had apples and pears from Aunt Lillie's front yard in Virginia. She also had a smoked shoulder of pork wrapped in paper and placed inside a burlap bag. This was the prized possession. Aunt Lillie had come to feed a hungry family in Baltimore. She was always right on time.

We couldn't wait to get her to the house. As she climbed the rickety front steps to 1641 Barnes Street, around the corner from The Johns Hopkins Medical School, she called out for the children to get the paring knives to peel the apples and pears. She called for the big pots to boil the water for the old blue Ball canning jars with the pinkish rubber o-rings. When

Aunt Lillie pulled out her white canvas apron we knew we would have tasty treats for the winter. Perched on the edge of a not so steady chair or an old Kohler aluminum tub turned upside down, Aunt Lillie would hoist up her dress a bit and place an empty pot between her legs. She had no shame that her heavy nylons, knotted at the knees, were exposed. When the children laughed about her stockings she said, "I am not here for a fashion show." With near lightning speed, Aunt Lillie began peeling apples and pears and in no time at all they were dropping like flies into the pot between her legs.

Talking fast while peeling, Aunt Lillie told stories of the bitter segregation in the South. I had felt it firsthand. I was with Aunt Lillie on summer vacation when a white bus driver told us to get up from our seats. We weren't far enough behind the white line that divided Black from white. He said we could not have two seats, even though I was too big to sit on her lap. He demanded that we go to the back and stand. Aunt Lillie refused. Egged on by other white passengers, the driver came to our seats and threatened to throw us from the bus. Aunt Lillie never budged. He shouted obscenities. Aunt Lillie shouted back. "I been baking pies and cakes for white folks to eat all morning. I'll be washing your pissy bed sheets tonight. And right now we gonna' be sitting in your white seats 'til we get off." With my heart racing and fear nearly choking me, Aunt Lillie turned my head to the window. We rode home silent but seated.

Hours later, and still in her traveling hat, Aunt Lillie had the apples and pears ready to be preserved. We were comforted by the smell of allspice, cinnamon, cloves and sugar; and with the sight of Aunt Lillie putting the big pot on the wood-burning stove, we all settled down. Aunt Lillie was back in town. She was our second mother. With the preserves bubbling and thickening on the stove and the Ball jars ready for filling, Aunt Lillie took the wrappings from the smoked pork. Slicing the meat like it was gold-leaf, Aunt Lillie showed us how to make it last for the winter.

When I learned that your mother might join you in the White House to care for your girls and to support you in this awesome job, I was ecstatic. Young people can always use a second mother. It reminded me of my Aunt Lillie coming to support my mother during difficult times. As First Lady, you will definitely be in exhilarating but difficult times. I am writing this letter for my Aunt Lillie. She didn't get a lot of schooling but she gave a lot of love. She knew how to be a second mother. If my Aunt Lillie was alive she would tell you not to let anyone push you around and make sure you take care of your babies. While your mom doesn't have to bring apples or pears in old suitcases to the White House, I know she will be toting bushels of love for your entire family. Written for my Aunt Lillie.

Warmly,

Peggy Brooks-Bertram

Peggy Brooks-Bertram is a native of Baltimore, Maryland. She is the cofounder of the Uncrowned Queens Institute and mother of two children, poet/photographer Lillian Yvonne-Margaret and international fashion photographer Dennison Ivon Jean Bertram. Her husband, Dennis Bertram, is also an artist. Peggy is a poet/playwright and scholar on the life of Drusilla Dunjee Houston. In 2007 she published a long-lost manuscript of Houston's, "Origin of Civilization from the Cushites." She is also a community activist with interests in the health care of African American women.

ADORATION

Dear Michelle,

i have dreamed many times of womyn like you.
i have often wondered what it was like to be partnered with
    a man
who is your reflection and the lover of our people.
Many moons ago,
i watched you date the Senior Class President
or the Captain of the Football Team in high school,
and i admired the magnetism of your beauty.
Later on in college,
i witnessed you get courted by the Student Government
    President
or the Minister of Information in the Black Student Union,
i was in awe of your irrepressible strength.
Then as i progressed through life,
i saw you shine through your own personal achievements,
and take on a mate whose "shine" you knew you could
    nurture
beyond brilliance.
i stood in amazement of your patience.
i marvel over your equation of success.
i ponder endlessly on your working formula for perfectly
    flowing love.

i dig deeper into my mental recesses
and ask how do you orchestrate your divine balance of
motherhood, daughterhood, sisterhood, womynhood,
marriage, professionalism, and faith?
How do you actually achieve being a domestic goddess and
a revolutionary at the same time?
Then i conclude that Sister Michelle is within us all.
When i behold her heights,
i am witnessing the magnificent rising of my own rainbow
    within me . . .
a wide, long, over-arching, blessing in the midst of
life's illusionary ceilings and rainstorms—
God's re-acquaintance with The Sun.
To thank you is to acknowledge all of our history's greatest
    Queens:
Great-grandmothers, grandmothers, mothers, aunts,
    daughters,
sisters, cousins, nieces, and friends.
As Afrikan womyn,
our heritage and pride never ends.
Our legacy is to know that we never walk alone
and our tradition is to defy being destroyed.
We have come so far
and endured so much
for so long.
Michelle,
when your shoulders are weary
and your back is resistant from the perseverance of
the mission and the movement to remain standing—
lean on me.
i am here.
The power of God is within us,
and the universe awaits . . .
"Ashay!"

"It once was. It is so. It shall be."

vonetta t. rhodes

vonetta t. rhodes is a resident of Buffalo, New York. She is a founding member of Malika Kambe Umfazi (MKU), a sorority that promotes academic, philanthropic, social, and cultural growth for all women of Afrika's Diaspora. Founded in 1995 at the University at Buffalo, MKU is a young sorority; its members build and foster knowledge on the value of women's work to reclaim the stolen legacy of Afrika's contributions to the world.

Dear Michelle, First Lady of the United States,

Almost thirty years ago, at age sixty-three, my mother "gave up the ghost." She was a woman who, when eight years old, walked behind mules to plow fields, rose at four a.m. to milk cows and possessed only two school dresses, one of which she washed nightly to wear the next day. When her mother died at age forty-one (in 1935) from pneumonia and childbirth in a cold North Carolina sharecropper's cabin, mother became, along with her father, caretaker for eleven siblings. Later, as a young bride, she would become a skilled seamstress, proud church choir soprano, and humble domestic servant, on her knees scrubbing white tile floors in bathrooms, tending curly-haired blonde babies and saving pennies in glass jars to make sure her two daughters went to college.

I am the older daughter, around the age of your mother. When I see you and your mother and your two beautiful daughters, Malia and Sasha, and understand that you have, with your husband, been chosen to occupy the White House as First Family of the United States, I realize that Heaven has spoken. Indeed, Heaven sings! Heaven offers a grace note to peasant women of the world and calls upon all those who are not peasants to pay attention. Heaven announces that peasant women should be honored and glorified for we are the viola, rosa, and hibiscus genera of the world, bringing

13

beauty and fragrance and a plethora of gifts for any wise enough to notice.

"For better, for worse, for richer, for poorer, in sickness and in health," you and your mother have been chosen to "sit-in" for my mother, for me, for my grandmothers and their ancestors, and for millions of other mothers, daughters, sisters, and nieces who continue to toil without benefit of respect, reverence, or just wages. Heaven has married you to the reality and memory of our suffering and to the promise of all our hopeful tomorrows symbolized by your husband's ascendancy to presidential office.

I never doubted that your husband would become the first African American President in my lifetime. Although I expected to be at least ninety-six years old, the age at which my paternal grandmother died, when Senator Obama won the presidential office. I give thanks that I am young enough to be fully cognizant of this historic moment and to share my thoughts and feelings of joy with you. I gain a mother's pleasure when I watch you and your husband together, your reassuring smiles, the way you hold hands and the other tender expressions of love that flow so naturally between you.

Finally, I cannot end this letter without letting you know that separate from my perception of Heaven's praise for you, your mother, our grandmothers and their mothers, our sisters, daughters, and nieces, I also feel the spirit of your father, Fraser Robinson III. In your persona I sense the sacrifice, dedication, and hard work that he poured into the upbringing of you and your brother, Craig. Your countenance, as well as your words, "he just woke up a little earlier, and worked a little harder," allow me and the world to recognize that you, like me and hundreds of other descendants of enslaved Africans, are the daughters of men whose love for family rose above self and struggle.

I give thanks for these fathers and honor their memory, for surely from their front-row center heavenly seats, they watch, smile, and listen to Heaven's praise song, knowing that their sacrifices and labors were not in vain.

I will continue to hold you, your husband, your mother, your daughters, and other members of your family in my heart, thoughts, and daily prayers. May God keep you in perfect peace.

With much love,

Jeannette Drake

Jeannette Drake is a retired Licensed Clinical Social Worker who resides in Richmond, Virginia. She is a writer whose work has been published in the Southern Review and Callaloo among others. Occasionally, she conducts dreamwork and expressive art workshops and is currently working on a novel.

Dear Michelle,

As a seventy-year-old Brooklyn-born African-American mother and widow who has spent almost half of her life on the African continent, I cannot tell you how proud I am to have lived to see you and your family arrive at the White House. My one wish would be that public diplomacy regains its preeminence in building and maintaining mutual understanding and unity in our foreign affairs.

Although I have had my own firsts, first in family to go to college; first African-American to live in Guinea, West Africa for eighteen years; first African-American woman to head several U.S. Foreign Service positions in Africa and India, I can't begin to relate to the huge importance of being a first on the world's stage. It is no understatement that women from all over the world, especially those in Africa, watch you and pray for you and your family as they pray for themselves.

My hope is that these women and youth get to know you and the President-elect as well as we do in the United States. I am sure that you have heard before that people in developing and less-developed countries who have spent almost all of their lives mired in tyranny, corruption, and despair, are joining Americans of all origins who are also destitute and despairing, in looking to President Obama. You and your lovely daughters are symbols of hope, beauty, dignity, and integrity. However, there are many non-English-speaking populations the world over to whom your message of hope and unity have yet to arrive. They were and remain of major concern to me. These are the people who are most vulnerable to negative attractions offering false remunerations.

As a former Public Affairs Officer (PAO) at the now-defunct United States Information Agency (USIA), which fell prey to the Jesse Helm's-led call for absorption into the State Department, I mourn the information and cultural exchange programs which so effectively promoted mutual understanding. Many of USIA's programs and products fell into disuse, unable to survive in an environment that neither understood nor appreciated the importance of public diplomacy among all levels of a host country's society. Our failure to engage these populations in thought-provoking contacts has led to greater misunderstanding of the United States, fanned by invasive anti-Americanisms. Unfortunately, the absence of USIA support in Congress also led to the funding for media-related and democracy-building programs, two of USIA's many staples, being given to another agency, USAID, ill-equipped to address the public diplomacy needs of these programs. Ironically, these funds were frequently locally transferred to PAOs to implement the programs, but with a more statistical rather than long-term benefit outlook.

I do realize that in today's economic environment, increasing public diplomacy efforts may not be a high priority, given our domestic problems. Nevertheless, I hope that it will be among the priorities because it is closely related to our security and antiterrorism efforts. And, just as important, is the fact the public diplomacy, well-executed by inspired and committed officers, generates a wealth of mutual understanding that is sorely missing from today's world.

My only regret is that, now retired, I am unable to support President-elect Obama's administration more actively. But, inspired by you, I will continue to use my limited skills to promote understanding and dialogue. Public reaction to my just wearing an Obama '08 button during my last trip to West Africa (Senegal, Guinea) generated smiles, positive comments, and untold assistance by all who saw me.

Finally, I again send you my sincere congratulations, as I join the millions of others awaiting your arrival at the White House of the United States of America.

Miriam E. Guichard

Miriam E. Guichard resides in Beltsville, Maryland. She is a retired U.S. Public Affairs Officer who served in Africa for thirty years, eighteen of which she served in the Republic of Guinea. She is working on a book based on her experiences.

Dear Mrs. Michelle Obama,

It is with the greatest of pleasure that I write this letter of encouragement and love to you and your wonderful family. As an "Uncrowned Queen" and a former U.S. Air Force child who had the opportunity to attend and graduate high school in Japan, I am so very pleased that you have chosen to make military families your personal charge. As a young woman growing up on a military base there was little opportunity to see role models who were aspiring to attend college. I was the only minority female in my graduating class and the first Black person to graduate from Johnson High School in Tokyo, Japan.

While I struggled to attend college as I raised my three children, I knew that I wanted to work in an environment where our community children would not struggle as I did going to college. I am currently the director of a pre-collegiate program at the University at Buffalo which encourages and prepares 7th-12th graders for a career in the fields of science, technology, engineering, mathematics, and the licensed professions. Over the past 22 years I can proudly say that we've attained a 100% graduation rate and 98.5% college admissions rate. Some of our alumnae are now practicing medicine, in various specialties including surgery, pediatrics, gynecology, and family medicine. Some have become scientists and physical therapists. Others are lawyers, social workers, science teachers, and librarians, to name a few.

I have been blessed to have touched over 2,600 lives over the 22 years and in this work, I am eager to see the impact you will have with your vast array of resources on these military families (especially the children) who need an advocate for all aspects of their lives. Once again, thank you for choosing to make the lives of military families a priority. I know you will make a superb First Lady.

Best regards,

Patricia E. Clark

Patricia E. Clark lives in Buffalo, New York, but is a native of Bermuda. She is the director of the science and technology enrichment program at the University at Buffalo. She is interested in preparing students to enter the licensed professions of science, technology, engineering, and math. She is the mother of three children: DeAnna, Devon, and Jaye. Patricia is also an "Uncrowned Queen."

Dear Michelle,

You are me.

When I look at you, I see me.

I see the young African American woman who, through good family values, strong roots, hard work, and perseverance, has come into her own.

When I look at you, I see my sister. The sister who I knew always wanted the best for me; especially when I made choices I had absolutely no business making!

I see my mother, a strong pragmatic, practical woman who knows how to keep it all together, even in the face of adversity.

I see the mother who always cares for and about other people.

When I look at you, I see my favorite cousin; the beautiful one whose skin and whole being always seem to glow. The one whose laugh and smile I always wanted to emulate.

When I look at you, I see my sista friend. The friend I can talk to, and laugh and cry with, about anything!

You and Barack, you are two of the precious few others who looked like me in college and law school. You are me.

Through you, so many of us see ourselves.

Thank you for allowing me—and the world—to see all of this.

I thank you for the beautiful face of black America you have presented to the world.

For all the history you and Barack have and will continue to make, one of the simplest and most treasured is your showing the world the face of black America; the beautiful, faithful, accomplished, nurturing, caring, loving, smart, strong, and moral face of black America. What a wonderful picture you have drawn for the world.

What a wonderful story you're telling.

And what a beautiful portrait of real love you have shown the world. Thank you for showing the world how love between a black man and woman can, and should, look. Through you black men have the opportunity to see the way Barack expresses his love for you; the way he shows his respect for you; the way he communicates with you; the way he allows you to be—to shine.

Through you black women see the way you do all of the same things for your husband.

Through you, we see how the two of you depend and lean on each other.

Thank you.

You and Barack, with so much history and the burdens of so many carried on your backs, have given pride and hope to so many.

Thank you for that.

Because you have given so much to so many, I hope and pray that you feel and are able to receive the encouragement and support of all the people you inspire.

As you and Barack carry the burdens that have been placed upon you, please know you are not alone. You and your beautiful family are thought of and prayed for daily by the millions you inspire.

Though your journey may not be easy in the coming days, weeks, months, or years, think of us to ease your burden and pain.

Think of those who you inspire.
Think of those who you have given hope to.
Think of those whom you have filled with pride.
Think of your sister.
Think of your sista friend.
Think of your favorite cousin.
Think of your mother.
Think of me. We are the same.

Sincerely Yours in Christ,

Lori Jones

Lori Jones is a resident of Bowie, Maryland.

"MOM-IN-CHIEF": MICHELLE OBAMA, MOTHER OF THE NATION

"Sing a song full of the hope that the present has brought us . . ."

Dear Michelle or "Mom-in-Chief,"

Your ascent to the White House in January 2009 as the First Lady of the United States of America fills countless women and girls around the world with great pride.

We exude pride because you represent both a long-awaited and exceedingly deserving *first* African American First Lady of this nation.

We are also proud of your expressed brilliance, particularly the manner by which you advocate the change we need in America and the world.

We additionally hold dear your extraordinary life accomplishments, including what you, a person of humble origins, have made of yourself and your family.

But mostly, we take pride in Michelle Obama because you signify our inspiring "Mother of the Nation," filling us with *Hope* by your enduring examples of *love-in-action* for your life partner, children, elders, extended family, ancestors, and fellow citizens of diverse walks of life.

Hope can instigate the healing of centuries-old wounds.

Hope can rebuild a nation in crisis.

Hope can restore faith in oneself and each other.

Hope can change the course of human destiny.

Be assured that the determined nature of your love-in-action instills *Hope* in numerous Americans and even others outside this country who observe, listen to, or come in contact with you.

For the determined quality of your love-in-action implores us to take up the task to define our nation anew when you ask: *What kind of country do we want to hand over to our children? Not just mine. Our children. Our country is not good enough for my girls or for any of our children. (December 20, 2007)*

Your love-in-action determinedly reminds us of our obligation to the aged who have nurtured us and on whose shoulders we stand: *Most of our seniors are not living with the respect and dignity that they need . . . I need my mom who is 70 years old and retired . . . And there's nothing like grandma! We need our seniors, whole and solid and ready to contribute to the next generation . . . (February 3, 2008)*

That's *Hope*, again!

Your determined love-in-action instructs us what Barack will do for the cynical, confused, isolated, and passive citizens among us to make change: *Barack Obama will require you to work. He is going to demand that you shed your cynicism. That you put down your divisions. That you come out of your isolation, that you move out of your comfort zones. That you push yourselves to be better. And that you engage. (February 20, 2008)*

That's *Hope*, again!

With determination, your love-in-action describes a path of resistance for victims of discrimination and prejudice: *Your voices of truth and hope and of possibility have got to drown out the skeptics and the cynics. (June 26, 2008)*

That's *Hope*, again!

You explain how to understand and emulate the determination of our forebears who bequeathed us a legacy of love-in-action: *(T)he 88th anniversary of women winning the right to vote, and the 45th anniversary of that hot summer day when Dr. King lifted our sights and our hearts with his dream for our nation. I stand here today at the crosscurrents of that history— knowing that my piece of the American Dream is a blessing hard won by those who came before me. All of them driven by the same conviction that drove my dad. . . . The same conviction that drives the men and women I've met all across this country. (August 25, 2008)*

That's *Hope*, again!

If *Hope* is to be alive and well, we must embrace the sanctity of all of humanity, across time, space and difference as you, Mother of the Nation, teach us: We are one another's brothers' and sisters' keepers.

Andree-Nicola McLaughlin

Andree-Nicola McLaughlin, a native of New York State, is chairperson of the Department of Interdisciplinary Studies and Professor of Women's Studies and Cross-Cultural Literature at Medgar Evers College. She is the first holder of the Dr. Betty Shabazz Distinguished Chair in Social Justice.

RAINBOW HOUSE

Dear Michelle

Never wanted
to visit the White House
till now . . .
now that you and your family live there
by proclamation of rainbow vote
and universal prayer.

I feel welcome now
that I know little girls
with double-dutch braids
and missing teeth
grow, play and dream there.

Your home feels warm.
now that I know
eighth grade student
Jacqueline Mendoza
will fly on nightingale wings
out of a forest
of wooden desks
from the city of angels
to watch you

and your man
walk into that house.

She too is filled with dreams
and she will dance
at the inaugural ball
wearing a red dress
made by her father's hands
hands that represent
a community in action
Si se puede.
67%
voted for change.
Yes we did.
We did this together,
black, brown, red, yellow, white
and 52% independent/green.

I hear the music of your bangles
as you move thru the halls
of the house,
the house I now think of
as the rainbow house.
I cry with Jesse.
We have lived long enough
to see
this part
of the dream manifest.

I smile with throngs
of unseen ancestors
of every hue
who have waited for your arrival.

They love you in red

as do I.
Please wear it often
it suits you.

Today's newspaper
deemed you and Barack
the most telegenic
President and First Lady
in the history of the country.
Appealing
to the eyes of the camera
and the viewing audience.

Yes,
you are beautiful,
easy on the eyes,
and so much more.
The thought of you
rests easy on my soul.

We see you.
My eyes
are the eyes
of my ancestors
and the great spirit.
We see your heart
and know it's goodness.

In the spirit of seeing
and knowing,
we add to the description of telegenic,
telegnostic.
Your vision
a country

whose people
more alike
than different
united for change.

You saw us whole
then challenged us
to stand up
in this vision of ourselves
and we did.

Thank you
for sharing your husband
with the world.
Your act of selflessness
has changed the course of history,
has enervated the cosmic DNA
and raised the vibration
of all life.
Harmonic balance is being restored.
We all breathe a little easier
Now.

Sequoia Olivia Mercier

Sequoia Olivia Mercier is a native New Yorker who has lived in Los Angeles the majority of her life. She is the mother of one son, Eric. She is a mental health counselor and R.N. She is a member of the Anansi Writers' Workshop.

Dear Michelle,

I want to congratulate you for the support you gave your husband, Barack Obama, to win the presidency. As an African woman I am so proud to see a traditional Black family settle in the White House. You portray the characteristics of a strong woman, sister, wife, daughter, and mother.

An intelligent woman would think before she speaks; you do.
An intelligent woman would see more and say less; you do.
An intelligent woman would hear more and speak less; you do.
An intelligent woman would protect her children; you do.
An intelligent woman would protect her husband; you do.
A wise wife would be herself because she is real; you do.
A wise wife will share her husband to save the world; you do.
A wise wife will love all people as if they were her children; you do.
A wise wife will work to improve the world for her children; you do.
A wise wife will love her husband even when they disagree; you do.
A good daughter is obedient and humble; you are.
A good daughter is loving and kind to all; you are.
A good daughter is happy and ready to share; you are.
A good daughter is willing to make peace with the enemy; you are.

A good daughter is dutiful and pleasing to the parents; you are.
A loving sister will hear the cry of the siblings; you do.
A loving sister will share her fortune with the family; you do.
A loving sister will look out for the good of the family; you do.
A loving sister will protect the jewels of the family; you do.
A loving sister will feel the pain of the brothers and sisters; you do.
A wonderful mother protects her children; you do.
A wonderful mother listens to her own mother; you do.
A wonderful mother hears the cry of her children; you do.
A wonderful mother respects the father and husband; you do.
A wonderful mother sings the praises of the husband; you do.
To you Michelle I take off my African woman hat from Cameroon, my motherland. You have given us African women the courage and the hope to move on and up. You keep your head high and hold your husband close to your heart. Keep praying my sister, you are the best. You have lived the dream of every ebony woman. Ride on sister, we are with you.

Ambrosia Kweh Mondoa

Ambrosia Kweh Mondoa was born in Cameroon in West Africa. She is an avid reader with a profound interest in cognitive psychology and black women in education. She spends her time teaching, counseling, and volunteering in the community. She lives in the state of Delaware with her husband, Emil.

Dear Michelle,

I've wondered how best to address my correspondence to you, our first African American First Lady of the United States of America. And so I say, thank you for your courage, intellect, leadership, and inspiration that have led us to a new dawn.

It is your courage that has made me mindful of my own. I rushed home daily during the campaign to listen to you and President-elect Barack Obama speak to a world that is known, yet one with immeasurable challenges. But you have stood courageously and have re-defined human values, family love and balance, and the importance of educational and intellectual development and growth. I have now found myself attempting to create a higher level of balance in my life and to think more critically about my role in life.

In fact, I speak with family, friends, my students, and others about how you have inspired us. Rooted in your work, we share our sense of inspiration. We tell stories about where we were when we first heard you speak during the campaign. We share ideas about your philosophies. We tell many stories about the day before the presidential election. So inspired, I remember setting my alarm clock for 6:00 a.m. on November 4, 2008, so that I could vote before going to work. But at 5:00 a.m., I was awakened by the thought of voting; I voted at 7:30 a.m. Watching television that night, we nervously waited, like billions in downtown Chicago and across the world, for the results of the presidential election. We discuss our tears and joy when, on the night of November 4, 2008, in the city of Chicago, you walked across the floor of victory with Barack and Malia and Sasha. I define this awesome moment as the path to dawn, Michelle. We rejoice because we've lived to see this day. We choose to believe that those who have left the earth know of it; that they are the twinkling stars.

Poetically, I feel as if the Ohio River sang that night; that the Nile kissed the Mediterranean Sea, the Congo had a meeting with the Atlantic Ocean, Lake Michigan waved, and the Mississippi wept. It is a story of stories that we will continue to pass on to the next generations. The experience reminds me of my poem entitled "Song of the Mockingbirds," and I share it with you. You are the song, you are the proverb, and you are the symbol of human dignity.

Thank you for the new dawn,

E. Rashun-Williams

SONG OF THE MOCKINGBIRDS

Sunrise opens her arms,
Draping her yellow-orange selfhood
in Mississippi, on the Mississippi River.
Silky, delicate feathers of the
Mockingbirds migrate. Liberate.
Grace-fan their purple-blue-yellow
red-rosy-white-brown-Black selves
over the river's silence;
history's truth in the palm of her waves.
Skywoman settles at Magnolia roots,
Her keynote written in the sky.
Listens. Conga deep-sounds oneness

for, all Mockingbirds have gathered at their nest.
Singing self-definition to the wings of Sleepy Orange
    butterflies.
Singing refinement to scrubby fields.
Singing wholeness to the foothills of open woods.
Singing self-affirmation to living streams.
Singing wisdom to wooded swamps.
Singing song-chants to the river,
honoring self, when midnight is asleep
nurturing their stories in her spirit.
I am. I am. I am the song of the
Mockingbirds. I AM.

Reprinted with permission of Gwendolyn Brooks Center for Black Literature and Creative Writing. E. Rashun Williams is a native Mississippian residing in Flowood. She is an emerging fiction writer and an English professor at Hinds Community College in Jackson, Mississippi. She has also taught at Tougaloo College.

HELIUM HOPES

Where do balloons go?
When we, celebration happy release them into
nowhere specific
Do they float to balloon heaven?
Where sanity doesn't exist except in hot air
And boyish good looks can still be gray matter

Where do balloons go?
After I'm sorry, thank you, and congratulations
Run out of gas
And begin to fall
Because I think I left something tied to my string.

Balloons travel to maturity
A wise woman said
Because the child will watch until the spot becomes invisible
And the adult will just know it's gone.

The adult is happy right now,
To finally live in a country where balloons can be free,
Dreams can live and never be guarded again.
Someone who sits at the helm of America
Finally looks like me.

And more than that,
The first family EMBODIES family,
To be a wife is a job I've trained my whole life for,
Being the virtuous woman, educated, refined, honest
and true
But to be THE Wife, confidant, primary cabinet counsel,
and support
Of Mr. 44
Who could ask for more?

You are my balloon.
Justified in the beauty your face displays,
Verified in the strength and authority of your speech,
Magnified in the reflection of your daughters.
You are my balloon
Hidden in the heavens
Now elevated so that my dreams may follow
And I thank God for you,
Prelude to dreams everywhere.

You are my balloon tickling the feet of God,
Favor filled,
Celestially covered,
And tied to my string
Is pride.

Andonnia "PhoenixSole" Maiben

Andonnia "PhoenixSole" Maiben is a native of Port Arthur, Texas. Andonnia is currently a graduate student at Texas Southern University, who has been writing poetry for fourteen years and is self-published in a volume entitled SANCTUARY: Serenity. *She is pursuing a career in higher education.*

Dear Madame First Lady,

It is indeed with pride and honor that I greet you on this historic day. At this moment in time, the world looks upon you and sees a new America, one of justice, one of reconciliation and one of unfaltering hope and faith in a dream that once was deferred but now has become its destiny.

On the great day of Inauguration, I pray that you be filled with the spirit of all the ancestors and all the thousands gone before who dared to dream of such a day. Be filled with the pride of the martyrs, heroes and she-roes who kept the faith on the long journey to freedom. Be filled with the faith of the faithful who through the centuries leaned on the everlasting arm and believed that "they that wait upon the Lord shall renew their strength, they shall mount up with wings like eagles, they shall run, and not be weary, and they shall walk, and not faint." For the days ahead will call forth your strength and faith and love.

Then in the silent moments, be at peace knowing that all that is was meant to be and all that is needed is at hand. Be assured that the hands of the Great Sisterhood stretch across the seas and across the eons to uphold you, gird you and lift you. And in lifting you, a people are lifted, a nation is lifted and a new world is lifted in accordance with a higher law.

Liberia stretches forth its arms. Africa stretches forth its arms to its sons and daughters in the infinite Diaspora. We

43

pray for one world of peace. Now, we can see more than merely dimly the fruition of what Dr. King called "the world house" where we are all brothers and sisters whose future is inextricably linked. Blessings be upon you.

Sincerely,

Teta V. Banks

Teta V. Banks was born in Liberia and grew up in the United States. She is an educator and a civil rights leader. As Honorary Consul General of Liberia, she is responsible for assisting in the rebuilding of Liberia.

Dear Michelle,

On August 28, 2008, my husband, Alexander, my daughter, Jessea, and I boarded a United Airline flight to Denver, Colorado. Our destination was the Democratic National Convention where your husband would accept the nomination to be the Democratic nominee for President of the United States that night. Since January 2008 when Senator Obama won the first Democratic caucus in Iowa, I had asked myself in complete wonder, "Could this be happening in these United States, in this country that has held out so much promise for generations of people from every ethnic group and walk of life?"

We were going to Denver because we wanted to be there when history was made. On this day, August 28, forty-five years ago, more than 250,000 people converged on Washington, D.C., for the March on Washington for Jobs and Freedom. Dr. Martin Luther King gave his memorable "I Have a Dream" speech and embodied a symbol that had long been a part of African American culture. He was the Dreamer. He dreamed of an America where his children would be judged by the content of their character and not by the color of their skin. On this day forty-five years later we were going to see the Dream fulfilled in the person of Barack Obama. He would become the first African American to accomplish what so many people of color could only dream of doing. We were going to Denver also because we believed in your courage and commitment to your husband's vision of a country and a world safe for your beautiful girls and worthy of the legacy bequeathed by Martin and Coretta.

We got off the plane, went directly to rent a car and drove to the hotel to deposit our bags. We didn't stop to eat, for the only thing that was on our minds was getting to the Invesco Mile High Stadium to see if by some stroke of luck we could get tickets to go inside the stadium. When we approached the area at around 2:00 p.m., we saw that there was a line of people that stretched from Colfax Avenue to Federal Boulevard. As we joined the crowds we saw that almost everyone heading toward the stadium had badges or credential tags hanging from strings around their necks. My hope that we would be able to get inside the stadium dimmed. However, we proceeded to inch along with thousands of other people until we reached the gate. Others who had come without tickets held signs saying "I need one ticket." "Please we need tickets for the members of the Alpha Choir." One African American man openly begged, "I need two tickets for my 'shorties.' These are my sons." A woman seeing our predicament said, "Don't give up. You'll get in. Stand beside me, I have a big voice." The line now stretched for a mile down Colfax, a wait of two or three hours.

Alexander looked for a place on the hill where we could watch the giant screen. However, we soon gave up and left the gate and walked back almost the length of the line to a place called Angel Mexican and American Restaurant. We were one hundred yards east of Invesco Stadium and we contented ourselves with being in this place that we now called "Angel's in Left Field." We were close enough to hear the roar of the crowd in the stadium and clearly see the convention on a wide screen projection as we sat eating our fajitas and drinking cranberry-pineapple juice. When we took our seats in the restaurant, the crowd was just beginning to gather to hear the speeches.

By the time Barack Obama made his acceptance speech at eight o'clock that night, the restaurant was packed with at least two hundred people standing, cheering, and creating their own magic.

Amid all of the excitement and noise, I saw my husband take a piece of cardboard that he had found on the table and quietly begin to write on it. He wrote in four columns the names of all the people he could remember who died before they could see the significance of this day: Lordell Johns, John Gabbin, Lee Gabbin, Sidney Williams, Ruth Williams, Jessie Smallwood Veal, Joseph Veal, Dorothy Johns, Albert Gabbin, Georgia Smallwood, Thomas Smallwood and Elizabeth Smallwood. As he wrote the list, each name was a litany that we would later recite with a prayer. It was not over. Barack Obama had been nominated as the Democratic Candidate for President. It would take many more prayers and a litany of names who remembered our scourged and embattled history to make this dream his destiny, your destiny.

When you and your family go to the spot under the shadow of the Lincoln Memorial, where Barack Obama will be sworn in as the 44th President of the United States, you will take with you our history of dreams deferred; however, you will also take with you our prayers and hopes for an America that is ready to build and dream anew.

Joanne V. Gabbin

Joanne V. Gabbin is Executive Director of the Furious Flower Poetry Center and professor of English at James Madison University. She has organized two international conferences for the critical exploration of African American poetry. She lives in Harrisonburg, Virginia.

Your Excellency,

It is an immense pleasure and honor for me to personally address this letter to you. I am a citizen of the Republic of Niger. It is the country with the poorest living standards in the world where traditional practices regulate the living conditions of most women. Violence against them is widespread and women's education registers the lowest rates.

I am privileged to belong to the educated and professional among them. I am an alumna of Temple University (Philadelphia) where I earned my doctorate in History on a Fulbright Scholarship. I have been an employee for nine years of the American Cultural Center of Niamey and have had good exposure to and experience of American life and values. I currently hold the position of Permanent Secretary of the Country Coordinating Mechanism of Niger CCM which works in partnership with the Global Fund to fight Aids, Tuberculosis and Malaria. I am also active in local and international civil society women's human rights organizations.

Since the historic victory that brought you to this highest position, I have been waiting for the opportunity to directly convey to you my words of love and admiration. I am therefore writing to congratulate you on this exceptional accomplishment to which you have contributed a great deal. I nurture for you deep and legitimate feelings of pride, fully aware that your leadership will make the difference for African women. I fully believe that your leadership will make the difference for African women. The journey that brought you to the White House has been particularly long and exceptional for our race. It has made women all over Africa expect change to come soon for a better world.

I share with others the idea that peace and understanding usually starts with personal contact and friendship among human beings and peoples. I turn to you to plead for the ending of the sufferings of our peoples and women everywhere in the continent, in Darfur, the Congo and in many other places including my own country.

I see the kindness in your heart that will guide you to accomplish many things in this world and to overcome all challenges and all obstacles. I see that our dreams and hopes will never die as long as we believe that you are up there for us and our children from all races.

I, and the poor women of Niger, have faith in you. We present this faith to you as a gift, the greatest gift of all from our hearts and from the bottom up, the gift of hope and love you rightly deserve. Your Excellency, I wish you all the best as you are about to enter this palace replete with the imprints of famous female hands and endeavours. I childishly dream of getting an autograph from you.

Highest consideration,

Zeinabou Hadari

Zeinabou Hadari is a fifty-year-old woman who lives in Niger. She is married with three children. She is the permanent secretary for the Niger Country Coordinating Mechanism for the fight against AIDS, tuberculosis and malaria. She is also involved with national and international organizations working to promote African women.

ANGELS FOR DREAMS

"I was grooming him to be President of the United States."
My father's eyes had that faraway look that for so many years
had gently and loyally cradled what Langston Hughes so aptly
called "a dream deferred." My father was lost in a deep memory, a vision he had held for my brother so long ago. The son of
Jamaican immigrants, my father was raised at the hem of wise,
but reserved, aristocratic skirts in the 1920s. Those women's
ambitions filled huge vessels. I'm sure my father gathered up
in his own tight satchel the counsel and good judgment of the
stately island women who met with my grandmother at her
house on Saturdays and Sundays, entranced in spirit tongues,
conjuring light to saturate the hiding places of those probable
demons of the early twentieth century.

But, thirty years after my brother's unexpected diagnosis
with a mental illness that spent and wrestled limp his keen
intellect, tight, quick body and infectiously winning smile,
my father quietly recalled in this intimate moment with me,
his earlier aspirations. "President of the United States," he
repeated more softly and wistfully. It surprised me. Not his
sense of great expectation, but the sheer, unabashed clarity and
magnitude of it. Frank and daring, it held no resistance. It was
not poised in defense against our five-hundred-year impris-
onment. Like those Jamaican ladies in our family, my father

had fully banked his own tremendous savings in the 1950s. Without a flinch or doubt, he had deposited it into his first-born son, whom for years he would recall with such deep sadness as having been "like a fine-tuned machine."

I've sometimes wondered how many others have had desires like this one for their own children. Not simply desires, but full-force outpourings of their life-blood. I don't know. I've never had children and will never have any. But you do. And so, I write to you with care. I write to you with a huge respect and a tender caution. Not to tell you a story of loss or pride, but to fill you with great fear of a God who gives and takes with ease. It is our inability to hold His magnificent garment and flow with the violent downpour that often renders us stiff, then torn in the end. Your dreams for your children may be somewhat different from my father's. Perhaps grooming them to be President of the United States is too small. Or too terrible, even. What I do know now is that my father was dreaming not only for his son, but for all of us. And so, his dream *has* come true. My prayer for you this day is that as your children grow into their fullness, and as you take your dreams, whether fragile, sturdy, announced out loud or barely whispered to yourself, and you hold them up to the light as my father has so many times over the years, may they be like birds on a wire, sturdy against the coming hurricanes. But too, may they be like flags blowing joyfully in the winds, with great velocity, no resistance, and carried to great heights on the wide arching wings and protective covering of the heavenly hosts!

Terry Jenoure

Terry Jenoure was born and raised in the Bronx. Her family is Puerto Rican and Jamaican. She is a violinist, visual artist, and educator. Social change, spirituality, creative functioning, and improvisation are all themes that feed her work. She is on the faculty of Lesley Graduate School of Arts and Social Sciences in Cambridge, Massachusetts.

Dear Michelle,

When I received an open invitation to compile a letter that would be included with other African American women all over the nation to share about this monumental moment in history, I thought, "What eloquent words or wisdom could I speak to such an accomplished woman?" I thought, "Why can't I call Maya Angelou for her beautiful words," wasn't there a card that said it all? As I thought more about my reservations, I realized that this letter was an invitation from the universe, calling upon my gifts and realizing that each and every one of us "are a gift." This was about a decision I was getting ready to make and taking a chance on the unknown ramifications in stepping forward and accepting this invitation. It made me stop and think about how many invitations I had declined in the past, opportunities I let go by, quiet fears and voices I listened to that said, "You can't." I am so proud of you and your husband's accomplishments, about being an American today, an African American woman, and there is more. Writing this letter to you is about a monumental moment in my history, in my psyche. If this is a pivotal moment or an "aha moment" for me, how many other people's mindsets have been touched by your gift?

To write you a letter meant that I was requiring myself to be quiet enough and truthful enough to sit in solitude to search my heart and soul, to struggle enough so I could place words to the overwhelming and smothering feelings and realize once I acknowledge my truths and fears, I could no longer rely on ignorance is bliss or "select" to take action. I would have to make a decision whether to accept this invitation from the universe and step out from behind my invisible veil where I could whimsically decide when to hope or allow my selected blindness to keep me feeling comfortable and safe, or was it time to embrace my fears and step fully forward into HOPE? How comfortable and stagnant has this mute, status quo position been for me? I realized that this letter was not only about feeling proud and honored about your courage, Michelle, but really a "thank you note" for sharing your faith with those you don't even know.

Yesterday during our church service, my Pastor spoke from the text in the Bible on Matthew 25:1–13. The scripture talked about how five of the women were "wise" because they had taken their oil lamps and oil with them as they waited on their bridegrooms. They had "hope" and believed that their mates were going to show up so they were going to be "prepared" for when the time came. The other five women were referred to as "foolish" because they only took their oil lamps but no oil. They really didn't believe or expect any change so they didn't prepare themselves by bringing oil with them for their lamps. They didn't have "hope." Once they saw the possibilities they then wanted to borrow some oil. They hadn't prepared themselves which meant they would miss out in some ways.

I am thankful for the reinforcement of the message through God's word, your speech at the Democratic convention and the outcome of the election to the universe, to "keep hope" and take responsibility to be prepared because we know change goes along with hope. Your entire family's decision on whether your husband would run for President was a testimony to this message: having the faith to hope and knowing you have to be prepared. The course of the election exemplified this motto as the nation watched. As I was leaning over to my twelve-year-old daughter during church service, whispering to make sure she heard this message, I thought about you as a mother and all of your private discussions with your daughters in sharing this message. Thank you for your courage to say yes, to step from behind your private veil into the public eye, to step forward with the grace of boldness, to carry a message that "Hope is a wise decision," and also for teaching the importance of learning to prepare oneself because with hope, things can change. I sat next to my daughter, praying that all women would tell this message to themselves, their daughters and sisters, nieces and neighbors, mothers, grandmothers, aunts, friends and sister-friends, strangers and mates. But most of all, I thank you from the bottom of my heart to remind me to keep being hopeful so I can keep flapping my wings and not be afraid to fly.

Thank you for being the messenger to remind us through your life example that when you have "hope" you can help others.

Sincerely, with a grateful heart,

Rosaria Love

Rosaria Love is an entrepreneur who is founder and president of her own consulting firm. She is an adjunct professor at Chestnut Hill College and Arcadia University, specializing in the area of gender and culture issues. She resides in Philadelphia, Pennsylvania.

Dear Michelle,

Please teach Malia and Sasha about the awesome women and men on whose shoulders President Obama and you stand. Deuteronomy 6:6–7 states, "And these words which I command you today shall be in your heart. You shall teach them diligently to your children, and shall talk of them when you sit in your house, when you walk by the way, when you lie down, and when you rise up." Please tell them about the daring individuals who braved hatred, ostracism, ridicule, beatings, and even lynching to give them and millions of Americans the privilege of dreaming and the "audacity to hope." My tribute to you . . .

AUDACIOUS
We Dare to Dream Dreams. We Dare to Hope.

Audacious . . . like the Birmingham, Alabama youth facing
Bull Connor's water hoses and police dogs
"HOPE so I could VOTE"
Audacious . . . like the Freedom Riders braving a treacherous
bus trip through the segregated South
"HOPE so I could VOTE"

Audacious . . . like Medgar Evers demanding, "If you can't
try it, don't buy it"
"HOPE so I could VOTE"

Audacious . . . like James Meredith embarking on a lone trek
to the Mississippi State capital
"HOPE so I could VOTE"

Audacious . . . like Muhammad Ali "objecting" to war
because his real enemy was at home
"HOPE so I could VOTE"

Audacious . . . like Rosa Parks sitting so I could stand in line
today and vote with dignity and pride
"HOPE so I could VOTE"

Audacious . . . like the Little Rock Nine walking through a
hate-filled corridor in quest of equal facilities
"HOPE so I could VOTE"

Audacious . . . like Fannie Lou Hamer enduring a deputy's
beating after trying to register to vote
"HOPE so I could VOTE"

Audacious . . . like Mamie Till opening 14-year-old Emmett's
casket and showing the world his mutilated body
"HOPE so I could VOTE"

Audacious . . . like the students from the North and East
coming south in 1964 and daring the media to report the
real news
"HOPE so I could VOTE"

Audacious . . . like Martin Luther King, Jr., dreaming of such
a time as this . . . when Barack Obama had the "audacity to
hope" so all Americans can live the dream so long "deferred"

Today, Hope Made Me Vote.

Michelle, God bless your family, and God bless the United States that President Obama has opened for all Americans. I, too, am proud to be called an American today.

Yours Sincerely,

Rose Parkman Marshall

Rose Parkman Marshall is a native of Mississippi. She writes and speaks about her experiences growing up in the segregated South of the 1950s and 1960s. She trained with poet Audre Lorde and novelist Rosellen Brown at Tougaloo College and was mentored by Dr. Margaret Walker Alexander.

Dear Michelle,

As I write this letter, thoughts of my father come to mind because today, November 22, is the ninety-eighth anniversary of his birth. My father, like your husband, was the product of an interracial relationship. Born in Louisiana in 1910, he experienced the pain and the ambiguity associated with the double jeopardy of being an "almost Black," Black man in America. Yet, he didn't allow the discriminatory environment in which he grew up and lived during the formative years of his life delimit his potential. His formal education ended after the sixth grade, but his innate intelligence, talent and tenacity resulted in what I like to call his being a "triple threat" man. He was an accomplished musician, a self-taught photographer and a man of the Gospel. And, I shouldn't omit the fact that he had a day job as a laborer at the Chevy Plant to provide for his wife and nine children. Like your father, he was up every day at 4:00 a.m. to go to the plant so that we could get the education he was never able to complete.

Why am I telling you about my father? Although we are twenty years apart in age we share a common bond as a "Daddy's girl." The fond memories, admiration and love that you have for your father and have shared with us are very endearing to me. I am reminded of my relationship with my father, and how much we all miss him. I also think that it is very important and instructive for Americans, who never knew, or those who never believed, to hear about the generations of strong Black fathers who supported and nurtured their families; Black men like our fathers, who, contrary to popular belief, were not absentee fathers and played a major role in their children's upbringing. How wonderful that your husband continues this tradition with your daughters and carries this message forward as an example for today's young fathers.

When I think of my father on this day, the ninety-eighth anniversary of his birth, I am certain that he would be just as excited as I am that your husband, Barack Obama, has been elected the first African American President of the United States. During the fifty years of his photography business, Dad photographed thousands of individuals, groups and events. His photos captured weddings, family gatherings, children's birthday parties, parades, church functions and organizational programs and have contributed to the creation of a visual historic montage of western New York's African American community. I know that he would be looking at the images of you, Barack, Malia and Sasha and composing, in his mind's eye, the historic picture that he would snap if he had the opportunity.

Michelle, our fathers are no longer with us physically. But, I believe that they remain with us in spirit and through the beliefs, values and love that they instilled in us. On January 20, your father, in you, with you and through you, will be smiling and proud of the history you've helped to create. I know that you've come a long way on this journey to the White House. And yet, in many respects, your journey has just begun. For the times that your way is complicated by barriers and roadblocks, remember to call on your inner strength—your father will be there; remember to call on your resilience—your father will be there; remember to call on your Faith—your father will be there. Finally, please know that I, along with thousands more of your sisters, will keep you, President-elect Obama, your daughters and family in our prayers.

With sincerest regards,

Barbara A. Seals Nevergold

Barbara A. Seals Nevergold, a native of Louisiana, is a lifelong resident of Buffalo, New York. She is a retired educator, counselor, and administrator for health care and child welfare services. She is the cofounder of the Uncrowned Queens Institute for Research and Education on Women, Incorporated. In addition to the Uncrowned Queens, her other passion is family history research.

Dearest Michelle,

I rejoice for you and yours for we are one. I am Crystal Peoples; I represent the 141st NYS Assembly District in the City of Buffalo, NY. I have loved your husband since hearing the brilliant delivery of his speech in Boston 2004. I, like most others in attendance, felt an immediate connection and sense of pride in him. However, to be honest I was even more excited upon seeing you walk on stage with your brilliant husband at the New York State Delegation breakfast the next morning. This, by the way, was the meeting I had previously planned to skip. I shouted and rejoiced more for you because it was like looking in the mirror. Not because we look alike, but because we are one woman, blessed to be born Black in America.

I have read every *Essence, Ebony, Jet, Black Enterprise, Vibe*, and every *Time* and *Newsweek* magazine. I also saw every network and cable TV interview you and your family appeared in. The love you all share for each other is both obvious to others around you as well as heartwarming. I see love and commitment in your eyes. I saw the cautious concern for your beautiful girls during the family interview on the 4th of July. Being a daddy's girl myself I feel the father's love when Barack speaks of you and the girls. This is the same love I saw in my father's eyes, the late Collin Jr., the same love I see in my mother Clara's eyes, the same love I saw in the eyes of my grandmothers, Vera and

Ella. It is also the same love I never got to see but truly feel from my great-grandmothers Josephine and Emmerit. It is the same love I have for my daughter and grandson. Our ancestors, yours and mine, left us the opportunity to make it in America.

My tears of joy when your husband accepted the Democratic nomination for President in Denver were nothing compared to the wailing flow of celebratory tears on election night. When you and your girls joined him on stage in Black and red I was awestruck. Wow, I thought, powerful colors for powerful people! I rejoiced for every little girl, every teenager, young adult and yes even every senior, who like me, can look at you and see herself. I rejoiced for the mothers who loved their children as much as you and I do, yet could not protect them. I rejoiced not just because America has finally elected the right man who happens to be Black. I rejoiced because I am you, we are one, committed to God, family and community.

Michelle, you and your family, America's first family, have taken a term from concept to reality. It is a concept we have heard most of our lives: "you can be anything you want to be in America." I thank God for you. I remain in constant prayer for you as you handle the most challenging job in America, that of being the wife of the President and the mother of Sasha and Malia.

Sincerely,

Crystal D. Peoples

Crystal D. Peoples is a New York State Legislature Assembly member representing the 141st District in Buffalo, New York. Peoples previously served in the Erie County Legislature. Assemblymember Peoples also serves on the NYS Women's Legislative Caucus and as an Officer of the Black, Puerto Rican and Asian Legislative Caucus. Assembly Member Peoples is not only known for her service across western New York, but also in Niagara Falls, Lockport, and Syracuse. She resides in Buffalo, New York with her daughter and grandson.

Dear Michelle,

When I was twelve years old, my mother sent me with a group of African American kids (with one white boy) to France to ski in the French/Swiss Alps. I didn't realize the significance until I was older that there were all these little Black "snow bunnies" in the Alps. I didn't feel special because to me we weren't. But that's the beauty of being from Chicago. I grew up in Englewood being raised by my grandmothers, aunts and uncles while my parents worked (and went to school); in addition to being exposed to the world. I learned who I was without the idea of the white man's foot on my neck, giving me the freedom to discover who I really was as a human within my Black skin within a multicultural world.

When I found out your girls went to Lab School (my alma) I was so thrilled. I knew you got it in a very visceral way. Attending Lab School was one of the greatest experiences I had in my life. Again, something I didn't recognize until I was an adult living in a world where the definitions of my Blackness came in a limited number of options. After going to Howard, moving to NY and working in film and TV production I began to see how others were defining me and I became devastated by it.

When I saw you, I knew I'd be okay. During this long campaign cycle, learning more about you and Barack gave me chills. I still get intense waves of emotion while unpackaging the reality of this new world. It's similar to grief, only I'm clear that it's a joyful cleaning out of old paradigms that had put a stranglehold on me that I wasn't aware were there. I hadn't seen how depressed and undervalued I felt until I realized that the whole world was mine again. I felt that what I had to say was important again and that now everyone would listen because of you guys. MARVELOUS.

What I really want to say is thank you for existing and remaining visually the kind of woman I've always wanted to be. I'd given up hope. I'd given up hope that Black men could affectionately and passionately adore a woman publicly the way that your old man adores you. I'd given up hope that I'd get to keep my booty and succeed in the commercial production world of NYC. I honestly didn't believe I'd be able to be intelligent and sexy at the same time and be taken seriously.

When I wrote my master's thesis on the visual representation of Black loving relationships in the dominant visual media, I gave up hope on Black love. It was the saddest, most depressing thing I've ever written. You two just blew it out of the water and now I have a chapter brewing in me about you and your old man that will be the light in the darkness. The passion you share with your husband always floors me. When I see him look at you and look for you. When you look up at him and when he touches you however gently, it is the re-ignition of thoughts and ideas I'd all but thrown out with the bathwater. It's the thing that makes me tear up even as I'm writing this now. You two have revolutionized what I believe to be possible in Black life. Black, young, sexy, beautiful, brilliant, and powerful. How marvelous.

Thank you for making me reconsider bringing my Black babies into this world. Thank you for being unforgivably Black and beautiful and brilliant. Thank you for allowing that man to love you and you loving him back. Thank you for being the breadwinner in your house and having your mother help you carry the load while Barack was off "community organizing." Thank you for those wonderful brown babies. Thank you for validating an underrepresented population of little Black girls from the South Side of Chicago who see the whole world as ours for the taking. And I promise you we will do our part in this cultural shift as artists and scholars to, as the kids say, "represent."

Sincerely,

Charity Thomas

Charity Thomas is a Chicago transplant bringing a hometown feel to Brooklyn. She has degrees in media studies and in film.

A CALL TO WOMEN NOW THAT MICHELLE IS FIRST LADY

Dear Michelle,

You are the one who points the younger ones toward the freedom of experience and I watch you from behind eyes that are learning and ears that regard the rise and fall of your ever increasing wisdom. My senses become sharper as I watch you weave in and out of life's dips and curves. When struggles come your way, you manage to get back on the avenue of life without making a u-turn.

I call you mama.

Your children are blessed because of what you do. Your maternal instinct has always been to care for the family as if they were your private garden.

I call you auntie.

For you touch others with the smile of friendship and your encouragement warms from the inside. You have the gift that makes me want to mimic your steps because of your virtue.

I call you daughter.

Your sense perception has been oiled with mother-wit. Love is part of your being. You feel and touch and taste deeply. From youth your naivety is just a passing stream of consciousness that develops into keen intuition.

I call you sister.

You edify, pacify and give. As I watch you, I know that I can say, I can do, I can be, I can desire and I can make things happen. My ear listens for your advice—because it sanctifies.

I call you faithful friend.

What you believe comes from a place so deep. It radiates out and flows like a river and you canoe upstream daily. You believe strongly in what you do for others and that belief is laid out like an array of floral essence. It's a contagious mission that will hold us together singularly and collectively.

I call you unity.

We have the same emotional traits, the same month by month calculating inner devices that make us women. We desire fellowship and truth. We desire it and serve it as a meal on a plate—served with dignity and grace.

I call you eagle.

Your watchful eye is on the prize. You seek opportunity on a road filled with the ancestors' sweat and tears.

I call you strength

You exhibit an inner strength to rise up and imagine that a better day is coming.

I call you rock.

I call you rock because you are solidly positioned on a foundation.

I call you mountain.

You refuse to be inconspicuous. You are learning to be unmovable and unshakable. You are seen as a force to be reckoned with—a force of nature—a mighty child of God.

Ashe'

I call you mama . . . auntie . . . daughter . . . sister . . . faithful friend . . .

unity . . . eagle . . . rock . . . mountain . . .

. . . You are all of these things and so much more. So dance, and sing. Sing love songs, move to your own sway, sing jazz, sing peace songs, waltz and samba to the calypso of joy and happiness, sing songs of our ancestors. Sing, dance and march to the rhythm of your own drumbeat—and the beat of your heart will be heard like a roaring elephant—and don't let anything stop you. For God's sake, don't ever stop.

Ashe'

Diane Williams

Diane Williams has been a professional storyteller for over sixteen years. She is the founder of the Mississippi Storyweavers Guild and the African-American Storytellers Guild in Jackson, Mississippi. She is also the Arts Industry director for the Mississippi Arts Commission and a speaker for the Mississippi Humanities Council.

Dear Michelle Obama,

To be honest, when my mother asked that I write a letter for inclusion in this book, I had no idea what to write. At this point, I am still unsure of what I have written. This book is full of letters from women from all walks of life, written with the goal of bolstering you with their words of courage and enthusiasm, and I can only hope that I have something worthwhile to add.

As I was thinking of what to write, I was listening to a recording of a poetry reading by one of my favorite African-America poets, Cornelius Eady. One poem in particular stood out to me that made me think of you, your husband, your family, and this time in American history. In his book *The Gathering of My Name* (1991), Eady has a long poem called "Gratitude" which opens the book. In this poem he describes his awareness at having "defied the odds," so to speak, when he says

[. . .]   Everyone reminds me
                      what an amazing
                      Odyssey
I'm undertaking,
          as well they should.
                      After all,
                      I'm a black,

American poet,
>
>   and my greatest weakness
>   is an inability
>   to sustain rage. [. . .]

Eady recognizes that to be a poet in America is no easy feat, let alone a black American poet in a time when the choices for black men and black women were still limited. Gaining [read: demanding] admittance into the establishment—any establishment—requires more than just a little verve and one hell of a hammer, and Eady can speak about this situation with even a touch of humor. He dares to open his book with an intelligent recognition that many of us would rather not think about, let alone state out loud. In his implicit and necessary questioning of the American establishment there is a refusal to be patronized, layered subtly beneath his wit.

> [. . .]
> I'm 36 years old,
>   a black, American poet.
>   Nearly all the things
>   that weren't supposed to occur
> Have happened, (anyway),
>   and I have
>   a natural inability
>   to sustain rage,
> Despite
>   the evidence. [. . .]

The poem's title, "Gratitude," invites us to ask how we can be at once thankful, aware, and productively enraged. These are the questions to be asked not just by African-Americans, but by all Americans, as we work through our many systems, most more than just a little clumsy and unequal. Eady says that "and no one / has to tell me / about luck", as luck is not the issue, despite how it has been phrased. His recognition of to where he has risen has everything to do with his willful defiance of [American] gravity. Perhaps American gravity is but an illusion that holds all of us down, boxed in the boxes we make for ourselves. Those who defy it and cease to exist within it will have both their supporters and detractors.

Surely, other letters in this book will contain words of encouragement written more eloquently than mine, so I will simply say that you remind me of my own mother, Peggy Brooks-Bertram—impossibly strong—and one of the two women who conceived of this project to give African-American women a chance for their voices to be heard, in hopes that you will hear them and from there, perhaps, the world will hear them. When Eady states at the beginning of his poem "I'm here / to tell you / an old story," this is what I think he means, that he intends to remind all of us of the stories and voices that shape all our lives, especially as African-Americans, and that his tale is but one of many that we have come to know. It is as recognizable as kin.

I know that you know how monumental this time, and your place in it, is going to be. And so my words of encouragement are actually borrowed, as they are someone else's words, but they seem to fit. I leave you with these lines, Eady's message to his lifetime of detractors who expected him to do no more than "drown out there." I interpret the image as being one of growth, progress, and the possibility of a bigger, more inclusive, house. These lines have inspired me, and I hope they will do the same for you and others.

[. . .]   And to the bullies who need
                    the musty air of
                    the clubhouse

All to themselves:

    I am a brick in a house
        that is being built
        around your house. [. . .]

In peace and strength,

Lillian Yvonne Bertram

Lillian Yvonne Bertram is a graduate student in Creative Writing at the University of Illinois at Urbana. Prior to college she was a Rotary Scholar and spent one year in Argentina where she wrote and published her first book of poetry, Tierra Fisurada, a book of Spanish-language poetry. Lillian's second love is photography, and she has published both poems and photography in literary journals, including Callaloo and others.

Dear Michelle,

WE STOOD THERE

As the mist rose off the surface of the great North Santee
With its twisted, mossy fingers straining toward dawn
You and I stood shoulder to shoulder on the banks
And watched them.
Dark men with strong backs and quick wit and gifted hands.
Mothers with high cheekbones and clouds of wooly hair
And the feeling of sweetgrass on their fingertips.

We stood there, we two, transported from another time,
    another day,
And watched as they carefully settled into their tiny boats
Stroke after measured stroke taking them to tend the rice
To hell
To the killing field

We gazed upon them, you and I, clamping our mouths shut
    with shaking hands
Fighting the urge to scream warnings of alligators,
Water moccasins,
Malaria moving mosquitoes.
But neither of us looked away,
Mesmerized by the beauty of their faces
And the new day turning blood red the mirror of the waters.

They stood there.
A cloud of witnesses; a million strong.
They stood there watching me, watching you
Watching over us all.

They stood behind your shoulder, to your right, one step behind
As you embraced him.
They whispered in your right ear as you whispered into his left.
And I heard a million whispers crescendo into a triumphant roar,
"Our daughter, we are O, so proud of you."

Tracy S. Bailey

Tracy Swinton Bailey is an educator and freelance writer living in Myrtle Beach, South Carolina. The mother of two and wife of ten years, Tracy was born and raised in Georgetown, South Carolina. An amateur historian and genealogist, Tracy has also investigated her family tree and claims ties to Hopseewee Plantation in Georgetown County.

Dear Sista Michelle Obama (aka First Lady),

Words can hardly express how elated, excited and proud my daughters and I are to call you OUR First Lady! On November 4, 2008, when the announcement was made, we cheered, shouted, cried, and prayed for you and your family. My 92-year-old father led us in that prayer, praying long and strong for you, your family and us too.

You know, of course, that everything you say and do or don't say and don't do, will receive intense scrutiny. Hah! I know that you are the kind of strong, Black woman who can take it all in stride. Like Mama used to say, "Chile, don't pay that no nevah mind." It's obvious to me that you know who you are and you know what you want. It pleases me to see you as the role model for Sasha and Malia, and so many girls and women who are proud to look at you and see themselves.

If you ever visit Buffalo, NY, you have an open invitation to stop by and chat for awhile. We'd love to spend time with you. Stay for dinner! By the way, I LOVED YO' RED AND BLACK ELECTION NIGHT DRESS! I know you took a lot of flack for wearing it but I thought it was supa-dupa-fly! Kudos to Sista Narcisco. Gurrrrrl,—I LOVE yo' style! Keep on keepin' on!

My family and I will continue to pray for you and your family. Prayer is the only real power source, comfort, and protection.

Peace and Love, Hope and Strength . . .

Karima Amin

Karima Amin is a lifelong resident of Buffalo, New York, who is the mother of three adult children, two daughters and a son. A retired educator, she is a Storyteller, a djembe drummer in Daughters of Creative Sound, an all-female drumming group, and a justice advocate.

Dear Michelle Obama,

I wrote a poem that I hope carries you into safe areas when the stress of the White House politics and protocol are overwhelming and closing in on you. Take this advice from this great-grandmother: Please remember in those times how important keeping in touch with the familiar aspects of life, that family will be your touchstone to reality. It is there you will find peace. So enjoy this new ride! I will be praying for you . . .

Blessings and Peace,

Andrea Barnwell

FAMILIAR IS THE FAMILY

Familiar is the family
The unknown exciting
Wholesome thoughts expand
Around early rooster crows
Unlike fast city black raven caws
Country birdsongs and railroad whistles
Dog barks and cooling fans usher in
New warm days.

New again this Familiar:
Family memories of waking to birds

That sing thankful to God who brings
Forth life abundant and good
Family thoughts of hopeful loving
Enter into each word given,
Each touch meant to flourish,
Grow, and expand, each deliberate,
Unending flow of the Familiar
Cascade like waterfalls rushing
Discovering new routes
Stimulate to jar senses awake:

Awake to the challenge
Awake to the necessary
Awake to the awesome
Awake to the wonder
Awake to new life

New again this Familiar
Chant of centuries old
Round song waking up the dawn
Closing out the dark,
Opening Up
Light-filled eyes!

Andrea Barnwell is a resident of Fresno, California. She has been a writer since the age of nine. Andrea also writes under her Ghanaian name, Abena and has contributed to journals and anthologies. She has received numerous awards and commendations for her body of work as an organizer, grant-writer, and mentor for faith- and community-based organizations.

Dear First Lady Michelle,

On November 4, 2008, the world witnessed the impossible. The United States of America with its history of discrimination elected a Black President. A Black President, who has a name that does not sound American. A Black President, who was elected by a majority of white people.

The United States of America, one more time, presented itself as a "big" country and taught the entire world a lesson that "what seems impossible" can be possible if there is a real will for change.

As an African woman, a French-speaking woman of multicultural roots (France, Ivory Coast, Mali, Benin and Gabon), I am very pleased to have had the opportunity to witness such an event. The American people should be proud to have overcome the deep differences in your society and lifted the heavy historical background that has weighed you down for generations. Finally, you have taken the necessary steps for the change you are looking for.

Barack Obama will not perform miracles, but the world knows that he is willing to communicate, to be respectful of other countries' values. As a result of these actions he will help to protect Americans.

President-elect Obama will rely on his wife to help him achieve his goals. Michelle is a wife, a mother, a friend and an adviser who is to be strong no matter what happens. She has already demonstrated this strength. She has shown women of all origins what it means to be a WOMAN, a WIFE and a FRIEND.

Through this election, the United States of America has demonstrated to the world that the American dream is still possible. Barack Obama represents this dream. Together, Barack and Michelle Obama represent the world: she is an African-American; he is of African and White-American origins. He could have been married to a white woman but his wife is Black, as Black as all the Black women in the world. Barack Obama's father could have been a Black man of the United States but he was a Black man of Africa. His mother is white as any other white woman in the world. This couple represents the dream of this century, the dream of millions of people all over the world.

In the most remote areas of developing countries people were praying for Barack Obama. The world needs peace, respect and love. We will all pray for Barack and Michelle Obama to succeed in this most difficult "enterprise." We pray that he will do a good job, that he will not disappoint the voters and that he will make sure that we never hear that it was a mistake to have elected a Black man as the President of the most powerful country on earth.

Black people of this country need to help the new President by having a positive attitude and by doing something with their lives. That's all he needs.

Kadidia V. Doumbia

Kadidia V. Doumbia is a professional dancer who was born in Paris, France. She has studied dance in France, Africa, and the United States. She has served as President of the International Women's Association of the Ivory Coast. She resides in Rabun Gap, Georgia.

Dear Michelle,

1931, Monroe, Louisiana. Magnolia Sims Frazier, a grandmother I have never met, was riding in the segregated section of a bus, tired, and pregnant with her only child, my father. The White section of the bus was full, and when a White man told my grandmother to get out of her seat to let him sit down, she refused. He began beating her, so badly that she finally took out a knife and stabbed him.

Well, that was unheard of in the segregated South, especially in 1931. The White community was quick to gather up a posse to come and lynch my grandmother. One of the local funeral parlors hid her, but the "Colored" section of town knew they were coming and were prepared. So prepared were they that the White posse thought better of it and didn't come.

Surprisingly when my grandmother went to court, she got off with a fine. Unheard of in those days when just touching a White person the wrong way could get you hanged. I can only surmise that the judge, when confronted with my diminutive grandmother, who was all of 5'4" and weighed about 110 pounds, heavily pregnant and being accused by a big strapping White man of being stabbed, that in his heart he really couldn't sentence her to more.

I never met Magnolia; she died before I was born. But her blood runs through my veins, and I've often wondered where

I got the strength to stand up not only for myself, but for the unfortunates around me.

Michelle, I'm so proud of you on so many levels; I see the strength, the self-confidence, and the love you surround your family and our President in. It makes me smile just to say it. Our President. I know your strength comes not only from your lovely mom, but from her mother and your mother's mother before her.

My father once told me as he was dropping me off at the airport on my way back to the University of Irvine that he did the best he could by his children by marrying my mother. He meant that because she was light skinned, which I am not (I take after him), we would have a better chance in the world. As a dark skinned woman in this society, and the society of the world, in every culture, the darker skinned you are, the more unattractive, the less dowry, the less choice of a good husband you will have. You see it even now in our athletes' choices of blonde wives, very light skinned sisters, anything but dark. You have no idea, or perhaps you do, how self-affirming to all the darker, less valued women on the planet, your husband's choice of you, a true, gorgeous, Black woman, has done for us. Suddenly our stock has risen, we are no longer immediately considered the hookers, drug addicts, easily used and easily thrown away as the movies, television and the papers have painted us for centuries. We are finally what we have been all along, beautiful. When I read the introduction of President's Obama's first book, *Dreams of my Father*, I was riveted by his comments about a young boy in your family going to a school and his classmates wouldn't play with him because his skin was too dark. I went to a Catholic school in San Francisco many years ago, the only African American in my class, and I sat for a year by myself at recess because the kids were told by their parents that they couldn't play with me because I was
Black. Don't get me wrong, I don't have a racist bone in my

body, most of my friends are White. I don't see color, never have, so I've been bewildered by it all of my life. The racial divides even in our own families because of our differing colors is sad. But you have gone way beyond all the pettiness and you are our model citizen and mother.

Have I mentioned how proud I am of you because of your education? No one seems to highlight the fact that you are an attorney and used to be your husband's boss. Guess that's a bit too hard for most people to handle. But all I can say is you both have rocked my world. I couldn't stop crying for a week after the election. I finally felt like a true American. When I said that at my job, one of the White men who works with me was very offended. But I have to keep in mind that he did say he was voting for the White side of Obama. But it wasn't just the election of the President, it was also that he had a gorgeous, strong, Black, intelligent woman by his side. He made my dream come true. And so did you by being there for him and letting him run. By putting your private life on hold for the next . . . at least ten years and putting your family in jeopardy every minute of it. You are true Americans. I love you.

Jacqueline Frazier

Jacqueline Frazier was born and raised in San Francisco. She works in daytime television and has received five Emmy nominations in sound production for Days of Our Lives. She also has written several episodes of the show and is a storyteller.

Dear Michelle,

Be patient with us . . . We all know you've inherited a mess of a situation and that there are no quick and easy fixes. We know the fundamentals have to change. We know change takes time. We know all these things and act agreeably when we're well fed, healthy and have money to burn and when we're feeling secure. Millions of us aren't, however. We're living in uncertainty without the loving familial bonds that fortify you and Barack and your precious daughters, wondering how we're going to make it to the end of the month. There will be those among us who will want to blame Barack for what he's inherited. However, the wise, sane, faith-filled and hopeful among us will continue to work in our respective states, precincts and communities for the change the country so desperately needs.

These are the best of times and the worst of times. I never thought I'd live to see an African American President of the United States. I knew if there was ever to be such a person, he or she would have to be wise, intelligent, diplomatic and a charismatic statesman, beyond measure. How wonderful, to find those qualities in a spouse. That's a blessing beyond measure. Thank you for having the audacity to hope with your husband.

One can only wonder what it will be like for you waking up each morning at 1600 Pennsylvania Avenue knowing that the weight of the world rests on the shoulders of your husband's Administration. The euphoria I experienced on election night remains tinged with anxiety, however, about his and your family's safety and well-being and about the monumental tasks before you. I continue to pray for all of you that the bonds of love between you grow stronger with each successive challenge.

During one of the darkest moments in my journey, in the aftermath of my father's death, I came across a poem that kept me grounded. I share it with you in hopes that you might find solace in it, too, as you live out this chapter of your incredible journey.

> Good timber does not grow with ease;
> The stronger wind, The stronger trees.
> —Douglas Malloch

That said, Renaissance Lady, Mom-in-Chief, keep keeping it real. Savor the moments. Know that we're behind you, alongside you, on the frontlines with you. Let us know how you're doing. And please, continue to let us know how we can be of assistance.

Blessings of peace & prayers of serenity,

Arabella Grayson

Arabella Grayson is an award-winning freelance photographer. She is also a freelance writer, ghostwriter, and editor. A resident of the city of Antelope, California, Arabella is passionate about the arts and has curated museum exhibitions based on her extensive collection of Black paper dolls.

NO LONGER DO WE STAND IN THE SHADOWS

Dear Michelle,

I have written you previously during the campaign, and received cards and letters of thanks from you and your husband. Permit me take this opportunity to express my ecstatic and overwhelming joy with the successful election of Barack Obama as the 44th President of the United States. This is something Black people never thought we would see in our lifetime. The joy of seeing the image of a happy Black couple, with their children in the White House, enthralled me. Black people were commonly portrayed as detached people living a life without care and having a welfare mentality. The only positive image we had of the Black family was The Cosby Show, which I welcomed with open arms. For Black people of my generation, it was all about FAMILY. The Black family was the norm not the exception. I grew up in a happy home with mother and father and other siblings. Seeing this image again with you and your family in the White House gives us a sense of renewed pride and hope. We experienced so many sorrows in the sixties wherein some of our efforts were thwarted and a number of lives that offered us promise were snuffed out. Many of us took solace in Africa and things African. Speaking as the person who created the system for writing music of percussion instruments of Africa, I have spent a number of years in Africa. I felt I had to relate a story to you and Obama, which I am sure you can appreciate. Recalling the limitations placed on us as a people, the train trips we took as children to the Southern states to visit our grandmother, leaps out. Even as late as the sixties, we could not enjoy the comfort of sleeping in the sleeping cars, nor eating in the dining cars, because of the color of our skin. Oddly enough the first train ride that I took where I enjoyed the comfort of sleeping in the sleeping berth and eating in the dining car was in Kenya, East Africa, the home of Barack Obama's father. I rode from Mombasa to Nairobi. It was 1970. It was indeed a joyous ride through the game reserve and I could see the giraffes striding, with their elongated necks and heads high above the tallest trees, off into the sunset. It was an image of majestic proportions. I often told this story to my students and they would sit in awe of my account. I would also tell the story and show slides of the slave caves that I have seen and visited throughout the continent of Africa.

I used to refuse to volunteer for anything, responding that my ancestors were slaves who unwillingly volunteered their services to free me from servitude. But all this changed when they opened a Barack Obama campaign office locally. I came willingly to volunteer, telephoning people, addressing envelopes and corralling unregistered people to vote, some who were voting for the first time and some who had served time in prison. It made me feel good to do so. It has been a long, hard struggle to reach this point. Retirement has come to my generation and some of us, who fought the battles, have passed on. Yet those of us who are still around are elated because we thought we would only achieve these heights in our celestial surroundings. We have now come out of the shadows, never to be eclipsed again.

The night of the election when the Obama family took center stage with Barack Obama victorious as the 44th President of the United States, tears of joy rolled down my cheeks. I uttered the words "it is a job well done," but my mother, if she were alive, would have said "nothing before its time." We are now out of the shadows.

God bless and keep the Obama family.

Doris Green

Doris Green was born in Brooklyn, New York. She is an ethnomusicologist, musician, dancer, and certified teacher of labanotation, a system for writing dance movements. A former faculty member at Brooklyn College and Teacher's College of Columbia University, she spent a year teaching in the Ivory Coast and the Gambia.

Dear Michelle,

I was so proud to vote for Barack. Prouder still, because you were there. Proudest, because you represent my heritage, my tradition, my hopes as a descendant of those who were enslaved.

Thank you for being such a personal, private inspiration for me and for so many others. While we were running for President, one of the great joys of this campaign was that it really did feel like "We the People" were running for President. You personified that paradigm of glorious women who campaigned in their fashion, for freedom, justice and the right to be.

Some of those who have inspired me are: Yaa Asantewaa, telling her men that she would go into battle if necessary; Harriet Tubman, and did she really say that she could have freed many more slaves if only they had known that they *were* slaves?; Ida B. Wells campaigning around the world against lynching; Aretha reminding us to *require* respect; Shirley Chisholm, believing that it was natural, possible and correct for a Black woman / Black person to become President of the United States of America; my mother, Thelma Biggers Redd, a single mother, leaving West Virginia, working as a maid in Northern cities, finally finding a family who would let her bring me to live with her and telling me and preparing me to be whatever I wanted to be. This enabled my husband, Ron, and me to bring our daughter, Mendi, into this world to prepare her to go forth and become whatever she wants to become.

The paradigm of excellence and inspiration has been in place for centuries. You're in that paradigm, Michelle, in full force: intelligent, witty, self-assured, caring, beautiful, respectful, challenging, inspiring. I am proud of you, grateful to you, and love you and your family. Thank you for being such a vital part of this dream that I never thought I'd see in my lifetime.

Love,

Shirley A. R. Lewis

Shirley A. R. Lewis was the first woman to become president of Paine College, serving thirteen years. Her previous experiences include faculty and senior executive positions at Meharry Medical College, Stanford University, and the Black College Fund of the United Methodist Church. She lives in Montclair, New Jersey.

Dear Michelle,

As you take on the role of First Lady of the United States, you also assume the role of being a representative for all the strong black women/mothers/daughters in this country as well as the Diaspora. Like it or not, many women will look to you as an example and will be influenced by the clothes you wear, your hair styles and the causes you champion.

I'm a young mother of a two-year-old daughter and I love that you have announced that your priority is parenting your two beautiful daughters, Malia and Sasha. I know that it will be difficult to keep them out of the glare of the public eye so that they have a sense of normalcy. Yet, you've assembled a team of specialists, your husband, President-elect Obama and your mother, to help keep your children grounded. Your daughters are blessed and fortunate to have their grandmother in their lives as her love, wisdom, experience and grandma "wit" will enrich and nurture their development.

In thinking about what I would write in this letter I knew that I would be among the multitudes sending their well wishes and telling you how proud they are of you. However, I especially want to commend and thank you for the example you've set and the message you've sent about the importance of the intergenerational bond between grandmothers, daughters and granddaughters. I know something about that subject because I've learned firsthand from my mother and grandmother. Michelle, I want to share a letter I've written to my mother, Barbara Seals Nevergold. It reflects my deep feelings about my mother and allows me to tell you something about her. My mother is one of the two women who conceived this book so that some "Uncrowned Queens could communicate to a newly Crowned Queen."

Dear Mom: I have always looked up to you and all that you have accomplished in your life. Your educational and professional accomplishments are numerous. Although you're "retired" that's a family joke because your passionate commitment to the Uncrowned Queens Institute means working long hours at the office and home, in addition to all your volunteer work.

At a time when interracial relationships were not as accepted, you married the man that you loved, ignoring the color of his skin. I'm sure you experienced your share of harassment and rejection. But the marriage has endured for 41 years! You had two beautiful children, me and Kyle, who you raised with unconditional love and support. You surrounded us with a very loving extended family, inclusive of friends, who never made us feel different because of our biracial heritage. Your parents were our loving caretakers before we started school, helping you to raise us as well. Oh, how we've laughed about some things that Grandma and Grandpa did that you never knew, like Grandma making us get our own switch from the tree so she could spank us. You said that's what your grandmother used to do!

Mom, as Grandma got older and sick I saw your strength and drew on it to be strong, too, so I could be there for Grandma and others in our family who needed help. I also realized that you got your strength from Grandma. She suffered many hardships in her life. Born and raised in the South, she married a man with four children and raised them along with five of her own. She suffered the death of two children before their time. Her life wasn't easy but Grandma was a woman of faith and her faith got her through all her trials. Mom, I know your faith also got you through the painful loss of your parents.

I always dreamed that Grandma would be here to nurture my children with the same love that she gave me. Sadly, she was called home before Naia's birth. However, I believe that Grandma is keeping watch over her. Mom, I have always felt I had a special mother. I've met many people who admire and love you. I am so proud of you. Although you've filled many roles in your life, Mother has been the most important to you and I have always been able to depend on you.

Finally Mom, the cycle continues. Naia has a great grandmother! If I can be nearly as good a mother to Naia as you and Grandma were to me, then I'm confident that she will grow up to be a fine young woman. She will have reaped the benefits of coming from a line of strong women who offer unconditional love and support.

Michelle, I just had to share my story with you, because I feel that we have a common bond in our values about intergenerational motherhood. Our relationships with our mothers and grandmothers undergird the relationships we have with our daughters providing positive attachments to cultural identity, familial support networks and personal development. By putting the focus on the historic role of African American grandmothers, you remind us and others that these relationships still exist. Thank you. And thank President Obama, too. His historic victory has made Naia's and other children's future brighter and more hopeful.

Sincerely,

Alanna E. Marrow

Alanna E. Marrow is thirty-eight years old and resides in Buffalo, New York, with husband Terry and daughter Naia. She works at a Buffalo General Hospital as a psych emergency room counselor. She also has a part-time position in a drug rehab program for women with children. She is a founding board member of the Uncrowned Queens Institute for Research & Education on Women, Incorporated.

Dear Michelle,

It's two o'clock in the morning on November 5; I hear the magic words: Obama is the new President-elect of the United States! I jump, shout, fall to my knees, start crying, then think about my ancestors, granny and grandpa, Uncle Jack, and all the ones I'll never know because of slavery. I begin to pray.

I ask the Creator for empathy, the kind that comes *not* from required diversity seminars, or college courses designed to make everyone celebrate something in others they don't celebrate in themselves. I ask for the kind that comes with our humanity. I pray for a day when everyone wakes up and knows we are our brothers' and sisters' keepers. An image on the news interrupts:

Cleveland, Ohio: The local NAACP office—Obama Headquarters. A room full of cry-happy Black people, tears streaming, all singing "God bless America, land that I love," an American flag waving in the background like it's Independence Day.

I ask the Creator for the understanding we're going to need from non-supporters as you, President Obama and your daughters, begin this journey in the White House. Understanding that as U.S. citizens we are connected by Indian land, a Constitution, and a series of institutions that have the potential to take us to the greatness those founding men, who I've never called "fathers," envisioned only for white folks.

I ask the Creator for strength, that deep down, never-give-up kind of strength that our ancestors had—the kind that carried my grandparents through a Depression they used to talk about. They were surprised they had kept home and family together, even when there were no jobs and grandpa worked for potatoes and meat, their daily bread.

I ask the Creator for patience to temper the jubilation everybody Black I know feels at this moment, our desire to dance in the streets, ride a roller coaster all day, stay off work for a week, call everybody we know to take a vacation to It's-a-Wonder-Land—that place we've all dreamed about, and doubted, and hoped for and didn't think we'd ever see in our lifetime.

I ask the Creator for safety, to hold you, brother Obama, and your children close and safe in everlasting, loving arms. I ask that each of you realize even in the most hectic, challenging, spirit-draining times how much, much, much you're loved and prayed for by an ongoing, unbroken circle of bowed heads and held hands.

I ask the Creator for a way to put into words the Aretha Franklin R-E-S-P-E-C-T I have for you—beautiful, brilliant, resilient sister—to let you know how much your husband with you by his side has changed my world forever, to share the joy in my 25-year-old daughter Michelle's voice at 2:35 this morning when she called screaming and crying at the same time to say MAMA, OBAMA'S THE NEW PRESIDENT!

Love,

Mary E. Weems

Mary E. Weems is a poet, playwright, author, performer and imagination-intellect theorist. She is an assistant professor at John Carroll University and the Poet Laureate of Cleveland Heights. Mary is a resident of University Heights, Ohio.

GIVE THANKS

Give thanks to the women, the mothers and sisters
who were there when everyone else forgot about you.
Who bathed you in their baptismal waters
of sacred nurturing, hanging with the weight
you suckled raw, cracked and callused.

Give thanks for all those midnight hours
they warmed your bottle,
the rocking lullabies,
the multitude of diapers unhooked
soaped, washed, rinsed and powdered
for your baby soft scent.
For all the days they bathed and clothed you
as you grew into your skin.

Give thanks for all the meals cooked,
doctor's appointments kept,
parent-teacher conferences attended,
the Halloween trick-or-treats,
birthdays, school plays and dress-up Sundays.

Give thanks for the mamas who never let you go,
even when they belonged to someone else

but adopted you as their own, no matter
what daddy was doing or where he may have been.

Give thanks for the grandmas, great-grandmas,
nanas, titis, aunties, lelas, maters and tatas,
the older sisters and sisters-in-law,
who took the place of ma to keep you safe.

Give thanks for those strong women who carried you
hundreds of miles over thousands of days
and wouldn't let you go, tired and weak, callused
and big-boned, bowlegged, overwhelmed and overweight,
hunched and aching, humbled and underfunded.

Give thanks for the ones who loved you
and didn't care that you were dark, or light, or fat, or young,
or old, or naïve, or fast mouthed, or cute, or fresh,
or silly, or smart, or pigeon-toed, or shy, or brazen,
or nosy, or noisy, or introverted,
or crying for something all the time.

Give thanks for every time
they went out of their way
to get whatever you needed,
begged and borrowed,
worked morning till night
to make you look outta sight
like you had more than you did,
and left themselves with less
so you could get a decent education,
who read you stories at bedtime
each night you lived in their house
or visited for dinner and slept over.

Give thanks for the dreams they gave you,
and the strength they instilled
in your will to believe in yourself
because they always knew you were worth
all of their love.

Sandra Maria Esteves

Sandra Maria Esteves has been a teaching artist for over thirty years and has taught creative writing workshops for the New York City Board of Education in addition to other programs. She is also a poet and visual artist.

Dearest Michelle,

Let me begin with this disclaimer: modern scientific principles, especially Black holes and string theory, remain mysteries to me. However, recently while I was traveling to work on the subway and reading the December 2008 issue of *Discover* magazine, an article discussing the anthropic principle of physics piqued my interest. According to the article, one interpretation of this principle states that "we are living in a special time and place in the universe where life is possible," while another implies that "the universe knew we were coming."

Certainly these words were not written from a theological context; however, by adding *Creator('s)* before the term *universe*, the revised principle states that it is the Creator who has made life possible and, of course, it was the Creator who determined our existence. And just so you know, this principle revision comes from a woman who failed the physics exam in high school but passed on her average. Nevertheless, as I fast-forward nearly forty years, I proclaim this moment as a wonderful time for this universal acknowledgment.

For many, including me, this special time and place in the universe has been defined by the election of Barack Obama as the President of the United States and you, Michelle, as the First Lady. On November 4, 2008, I, too, stood proud to be an American. I salute you, Michelle.

Statuesque.
Exemplifying respect,
Honesty and discretion.
Self-defined.
Exuding knowledge
And determination.
Self-assured.
Valuing the path
and the journey.
Blessed.
Woman, daughter,
Wife, mother
The First Lady.

Sharon R. Amos

Sharon Amos is an associate professor of English at the University at Buffalo Educational Opportunity Center in Buffalo, New York. She is an author, poet, and avid reader.

Dear Michelle,

I first became aware of the power of politics and the power of the people on my ninth birthday. On April 4, 1968, I was celebrating my ninth birthday party with friends and family in our Chicago apartment, when my father came home from work in tears. I had never seen him cry before so I was acutely aware of every single word uttered and every deed that took place that evening.

The scene inside our second-floor apartment was one of sadness. Tears and prayers flowed as parents came to pick up their children from the interrupted birthday party. Shadows formed from candlelight in each room as well as the gray glow of the black and white images emerging from the television: Martin gunned down on a motel balcony in Memphis. Mom uttered," . . . a dream deferred."

From our second-story window, I watched a different scene unfolding on the streets of our west side neighborhood. Fury and frustration ignited fires that blazed through the night. I woke to the stench of a burned neighborhood that was now occupied by the National Guard. I worried about my parents whose sadness seemed larger than anything God could fix. And I had been raised to believe that God could fix anything.

Forty years later, as I listened to your husband, our President-elect Barack Obama, declare that change had come to the

United States of America, I cried. I cried for the little girl forty years ago, who didn't even get a birthday wish. However, I also cried in joy for every nine-year-old girl alive today. I know that somewhere in America, there is a little girl who is blowing out birthday candles, wishing to be the next President of the United States. Her dream will not be deferred, but by all means can be, and will be delivered!

Living the Dream,

Faith Davis

Faith Childs-Davis is a writer, artist, mom, and arts educator. She lives in Los Angeles where she maintains a garden, a career in the arts, and a place in the hearts of loved ones.

BECAUSE OUR MOTHERS PRAYED: LETTER-POEM TO MICHELLE

Michelle, as you enter halls redolent
with the sweat and aromas
of ancestors unfree—
Griot walls that, if asked,
can tell the secrets of nations

Remember,
you are there because Our Mothers prayed.
Because Our Mothers prayed, you are there.

Mothers' prayers reverberating
through time from underneath sweating earth
upon which our shackled feet were marched
into barracoons, aboard ship, below deck
across the Middle Passage.

Prayers that echo
beyond branding blocks & auction blocks
between whipping posts & bed posts
outside groves, away from prying ears
on Watch Nights, into New Years
beneath retreating moons
despite bombed churches.

The prayers of Mothers uttered
over the bodies of babies
above washboards and floorboards,
inside jail cells and revival tents
along freedom trails,
throughout voting booths.

Our Mothers prayed, Michelle
words filled with spirit
poured into the fingertips
of clasped palms extended
arched backs onto which the story of 400 years
is inscribed in welt and sorrow
bodies frail but resolute
on knees, bent and bruised
propped by feet, sore and calloused
this is the bridge across which you've come.

You are there, because Our Mothers prayed, Michelle
because Our Mothers prayed, you are there.

Remember.

Amira Davis

*Amira M. Davis is a doctoral student in Educational Policy Studies at the
University of Illinois-Urbana/Champaign.*

Dear Michelle,

First there was disbelief, then excitement, triumph and joy, as I listened to the final, emotional call of the election on November 4, 2008: "Senator Barack Obama has been elected the first African-American President of the United States!" In a state of shock, I watched as newscasters of every creed were overcome with excited jubilation. It seemed that they too couldn't believe that they would have lived to broadcast the outcome of such a monumentally historic election. They had lost all journalistic objectivity in that instant!

I watched as millions of people of all races, ages, creeds and beliefs came together in a Chicago park, running to the stage as if their lives depended on it, to see their candidate in victory. And as the entire nation waited with baited breath to see our new President-elect make his victory speech, the moment that I had only imagined became a reality. I thought surely the tears would flow. Michelle, as you took that stage with Barack and your daughters, I was suddenly struck with the realization that it wasn't just Barack who had won the cause for "change." You were there with him, supporting him every step of the way and sharing his victory. Equipped with that understanding, the tears finally streamed down my face.

I realized that my sons would have the opportunity to see an African-American man entrusted with the highest office of the land. Moreover, my daughter would soon learn about the wife at his side, who broke stereotypes about African-American women and helped her husband to fulfill the hopes and dreams of so many.

Millions of American women travel an everyday, unhistoric, journey. They manage their families and work, if necessary, to support those they love. Often that work is in a world dominated by men. African-American women have the added daily burden of working to shatter old stereotypes, constantly proving that they can and want to achieve. These are attributes that you embody Michelle, and now they are put on display for the entire world! How awesome!

As a young African-American wife and working mom, I aspire to become the model that you represent. At home, I work to support my husband and nurture my children. At work, I hope to shatter the misconceptions of some about my morals, hopes, beliefs and abilities. So far so good! But I can only reeducate a few. I pray that having you as our First Lady in the White House will not only reach those who have the wrong idea about us, but will also inspire those of us who have the wrong idea about ourselves. Achievement is attainable by all. I hope that your tenure in Washington will spur a movement in the African-American community that helps to engender self-love and self-determination.

Michelle, you are an inspiration. I pray that the next four years (and beyond!) will be all that you hope it to be. And I pray that God will bless you and Barack with the ability to do the work that you set out to do so long ago on Chicago's South Side. We'll be watching . . . with baited breath.

With Love,

Nicole J. Day

Nicole J. Day is a native of Buffalo, New York. For the past thirteen years, she has lived in Atlanta, Georgia, with her husband, Marlon, and children, Miles, Mason, and Morgan. She is a marketing consultant to a human resources firm and secretary for her church.

Dear First Lady Michelle Obama,

Words alone cannot express the joy, happiness and gratitude I have just for you being your own wonderful self.

The manner in which you have supported your husband, President-elect Barack Obama; nurtured your children, Malia and Sasha; and cherished your mother, Mrs. Marian Robinson, during this spectacular journey is awesome.

You exhibited such grace through the many months leading up to that most eventful day of November 4, 2008. When the powerful news came through at 11:30 p.m. EST advising us that Senator Barack Obama was going to be our 44th President of the United States, there was such sheer delight. I was screaming, crying, jumping up and down, running up and down the stairs and thanking God for bestowing us with such jubilant news! I also thought of you, and how proud you had to be of that day.

As a divorced/single working mom, I can relate to the struggle to balance family and work responsibilities. I commend you as I know maintaining this balance is not easy. I have no doubt that your plans to assist divorced and/or single working mothers and military wives will bring about positive change in the lives of these women. I am so encouraged to know that you will be focusing on this cause. We need all the help we can get. I am not naïve as I know there are many other challenges that will require your attention, but I do think that you will make significant contributions in this area.

I pray that with the continued blessings of God, you will continue to be a tower of strength to your family and to our nation. Please be reminded that you will always have our positive thoughts and prayers. We are with you. We are so blessed to have you, a beautiful, intelligent, and graceful wife, mother, daughter, as our very own sister and First Lady.

Respectfully,

Juanita Dennis

Juanita Dennis lives in Spring Valley, New York. She is the proud mother of a daughter and son. She also has a precious granddaughter and her 92-year-old Nana. She has a wonderful job working at a leading publishing company.

HONOR . . .

Thank you, First Lady Michelle for epitomizing such a tall order:
Honor thy father and thy mother!

From sharing precious memories that you paint of a loving and
supportive Dad

To including your dear Mother inside the White House

Family makes a real home glad.

Thanks to your chosen path, precious girls like yours, my two
granddaughters and females worldwide are poised to take
uncharted leaps;

For we all are daughters of Abraham to whom much is
promised Watch future generations reap!

   With Love,

   Geraldine-Drake Hawkins

*Geraldine-Drake Hawkins, a senior program analyst in federal service, has
impacted thousands of public school and undergraduate students across three
decades as an educator/program evaluator. She resides in Bowie, Maryland.*

Dear Michelle Obama,

You must know the pride we feel for you, becoming our first African-American "First Lady." You bring great joy to women all over the world, not just African-American women. Not only are you an educated woman who has attended prestigious universities, but also you came into the urban community helping to uplift ordinary people. You are the epitome of the phrase "to reach one is to teach one."

Whenever I read articles describing your life, the one word I have seen most often is "community." I am the President of the Mary B. Talbert Civic & Cultural Club. Our motto is "Lifting As We Climb," which seems to be yours too. I was overwhelmed when I read about your journey from Princeton and Harvard Law to local communities where you created programs helping children read, encouraging people to volunteer, recruiting Black undergrads to Harvard Law and uplifting families in the community.

As your husband becomes our President and leader, we know that with each step he takes, he has you beside him; his rock and strength. Every successful man needs someone of your grace, personality and faithfulness. You have a charismatic presence; a quiet strength that exudes real hope that we can make this a better world, one person at a time.

The love we see within your family is awesome. We realize no family is perfect, but yours is so close. You and Obama let the world see that people of color have strong family ties, love that is not hidden, faith in God, who guides, and respect for all people. You show this love in the way you look at each other and even the touch of your hands especially the "fist bump." Then you add that touch of humor that makes us smile or even laugh.

The Lord has blessed you with a loving, strong family. We see it on the faces of Sasha and Malia, as they smile and wave at us, showing their graciousness that is guided by loving, but disciplined hands. But you know what I truly respect you for? It is that you have let us see your husband as a man, who is not perfect because he is human, like us. Moreover, you are keeping your children grounded by making sure they will still have chores to do, like making their beds.

I also thank you for your commitment to support military families, help working women balance work and family and National Service. These issues are so important in strengthening the family, which is the core of building communities and giving us national pride by serving our country. You are giving us hope for a future my grandkids can believe in.

My 88-year-old father said, "Never in my lifetime did I think we would have a leader in the White House who looked like me. That man makes me so proud and he's got a pretty wife and some cute kids too."

May the Lord protect you and guide you to the right path. My prayers and support are with you and your family.

Peace and Love,

Priscilla Y. Hill

Priscilla Y. Hill is a retired educator and writer of poetry and short stories. She is president of the Mary B. Talbert Civic and Cultural Club in Buffalo, New York.

Dear Michelle,

Congratulations as you approach your distinguished role, First Lady of our country. As your footsteps lead to the White House they leave on our hearts and in our minds imprints of inspiration and aspiration. The spirit of the place and people from whence you come shout, inaudibly, "Keep shining our brilliant North Star." We are traces of those spirits and perceive that brilliance. Our hopes are illuminated, dreams revived, and spirit of unity incited.

You exemplify beautifully the resilience, pride, and humility of our heritage. Our historical experience is above belief. Your authenticity portrays aspects of humanity that, in my opinion, society has been lacking.

May your moments of apprehension be eclipsed by your awareness of the adoration, respect and hope that encompasses you.

From prelude to encore, your reign is embraced with deep emotion, enormous gratitude and showers of prayers.

Sincerely,

Lily Parker

Lily Parker is a native of Karnack, Texas, and now resides in Houston. She is a career teacher, avid reader, and an ardent shell collector. Lilly gardens, erratically. She was blessed to be a messenger through voice and song.

SO MUCH OF THE WOMAN I AM

Up from the pine trees and the tall grass
And the seaweeds surrounding the
Gullah peoples in a little town in the south,
Sprang forth a humanity that is
Deep in you.

Into the hallowed hallways
And the sterile rooms
And the stately facades preserving the
Privileged in ivy buildings up north
You revealed an intelligence that is undenying.

Back on the home front and the busy streets
And the daily duties of a professional, wife, mother, daughter,
Sister, friend
You found a way to gracefully bring balance and beauty
To a world that is sometimes cold and unforgiving.

For so many, you paint a different picture;
Tell another story.
For me, you represent so many of the women I know,
So much of the woman I am.

The powerful, queen, warrior-mothers of the past are within you
And they are proud.
The favored children of the future are within you
And they are blessed.
The visionary, hardworking, and strong Black women of
    today are within you
And we are thankful.

So much of the woman you are—
We are.
So much of the elegance, dignity, strength, and character you
    display
We see everyday in ourselves.

When the days become endless and dreary,
And the weight seems too hard to bear
Look in the mirror and see all of the women who have come
    before you
And made it under dreadful circumstances.
See all of the children who have yet to come, and know you
    shine a light so bright that will make their world a more
    livable place.
See me—cheering you on, giving you hope, holding your
    hand, reminding you daily that Strong women keep
    getting stronger.

At the end of the day, when the outside world is gone, it
    is you who must decide to hug your children, kiss your
    husband, respect your mother, protect your family and
    love yourself.

And at the end of the day, when the world outside is gone,
Please always know,
So much of the woman you are, I am.

And I am here . . .
Sending you love.

Donna Aza Smith

Donna Aza Smith grew up in the low country of South Carolina. She is an engineer and is currently a consultant residing in Washington, D.C. She weaves words the way her grandparents weaved sweetgrass baskets. She combines her career and life experiences to captivate, enlighten, and inspire with her poignant style.

A CONSCIOUSNESS OF CHANGE
To Our First Lady Michelle Obama,

You bring life to a land by carving out the middle to make use of its heart in order to hear the sweet laughter of our children.

The liquid life is the heart of this land, giving shelter to all who seek it, for between each of us there is only light.

You walk with strong shoulders. "What would I be if I didn't make this land better."

Your face is bold and silent, graceful and constant, that brings light where there is darkness. Surrounded by fear while making the best in others rule, relying on the goodness of our world for the world must decide.

Leading a dream of change answering the call for peace while remaining in the still place above conflict and the acts of war. Your qualities will be known to your enemies wherever you meet them.

The light that shines behind you is not a mirage: it brings peace, a consciousness that brings an oath to safeguard the helpless, to protect the people. Be without fear in the face of those who question your oath, be brave and upright so that the Universe may love you, speak the truth even if it's the only voice heard.

Barbra J. Fletcher Stephens

Barbra J. Fletcher Stephens resides in Buffalo, New York. She is an Associate Dean at Empire State College of New York. She serves her community as an educator, offering the gifts passed on to her from her large extended family of life.

Dear Michelle,

It's 7 a.m. Thanksgiving morning and I just put my turkey in the oven and my ham on to boil, thinking, of course, about all the things I'm thankful for in my life. Though everything is not as I hoped, dreamed, planned, or even endeavored, I am thankful. I thought about how thankful I am for our President-elect, and my mind immediately turned to the email I received two days ago about writing letters to Michelle, and I thought:

Michelle, thank you for not embarrassing your mama. Every time you do your mama proud, you make us all proud. Being a tall sister, probably tall as a young girl, I'll bet your mama always reminded you to stand up straight! Michelle, thank you for standing up straight, tall in dignity, tall in integrity, tall in pride. You stand for those of us whose legs have been weak and shaky, and we haven't made it as far as we would've liked. You stand for those of us whose legs have been intentionally and unintentionally knocked from under us, so we just haven't been able to pull ourselves up, but we're still trying and trying to make sure our daughters and granddaughters are able to. You stand for those of us whose legs were simply missing at birth and will always need someone to stand on our behalf. Thank you.

Michelle, I can just hear your mama telling you to just be yourself! Thank you, Michelle, for not minding being one of us, for not having a problem saying you are one of us. Thank you for knowing that there are millions of us, like you. Thank you for knowing that you stand in the spotlight on behalf of us, on behalf of those who could never have conceived of one of us in the White House or any other house. Thank you for withstanding the spotlight that brings with it compliment and criticism, honor and offense, love and loathing. Thank you, Michelle, you and your beautiful daughters, for taking the blows with the blessings.

My mama left this earth when I was very small, but I always imagined she would tell me what I'll bet your mama told you, maybe not realizing exactly what she was saying, "You can be anything you wanna be." Thank you, Michelle, for showing us and the world who we truly are, what our creator intended of us, who we are and who we are becoming: mothers, daughters, granddaughters, aunts, cousins—First Ladies—standing tall, proud, moral, intelligent, compassionate—First Ladies—not minding, not ashamed, not rejecting, not minimizing that you are African American—First Ladies. I know that you and yours are not ours alone, that you are the standard bearers of a nation, indeed, a world that is waiting, watching, wondering: "Can any good thing come out of Nazareth?" Sister, surely you know, you are that good thing. You were chosen for this moment in time. Thank you for hearing and heeding the call.

Today, I will pray for you and your family, and I will thank God for you. You do us proud!!! Thank you, Michelle.

Respectfully,

Norma J. Thomas

Norma J. Thomas is a native and resident of Houston, Texas. She is a teacher of speech communications and theatre arts in Houston Public Schools. She is a producer, director, playwright, screenwriter, and spoken word artist. Norma is mother of Kam Enita and doting grandmother of Kamiliyah Mahira and Leelah Imani.

Dear Michelle,

Well, you did it. You kept the home fires burning, did not skip a beat doing the Mom thing, and stood by your man until the finish. Now you are going to reap the benefits. I know you are thinking, it has just begun and you are so right. The battle is going to be long and arduous and often unpleasant. You might scratch your head and say, "Did I really sign up for this?" First Lady, you should know you have loads of support, more than you may realize. There are so many women (men too) who have your back and want to see this new administration succeed and prosper.

Actually, when I read your life story and that of your husband, the President-elect—doesn't that sound good?—I feel as if this was a natural progression of things; just the way it was supposed to be. How can your story be any more American than a child of the South Side of Chicago, raised by God-fearing, hard-working parents who believed in the American dream? Your family reflects the millions of other families in this country, who migrated from the Southern states, who toiled in factories, hospitals, military bases, government jobs, and other folks' homes to put food on the table, made a home for their children and then went on to educate them, thus having faith that they would reap the benefits of their hard work.

President Obama's story is equally compelling, a true reflection of the amalgam of cultures that has made America what it is. That is why your family was embraced by so many; people saw themselves and the connection was instantaneous. Additionally, when women see you, Michelle, they see a woman who is secure in herself, her life, and her marriage. A woman who was secure enough to not step back to allow her man to pursue his dream, but a woman brave and secure enough to step forward and take the mantle of hope to walk beside her man to reach for the prize together. You knew what it took to make it happen and you decided to DO IT!

To paraphrase Brother Langston Hughes, life ain't going to be no crystal stair. The walk will get rough, the path will be uneven, and you may get a few pebbles in the soles of your feet, but I believe, along with millions of others, that you will continue to walk straight, strong and true, representing for all of us who believed it could be done.

God bless you and your family,

Dera R. Williams

Dera R. Williams lives, works, and plays in Oakland, California, where she is employed at a local community college. A writer, reader, and genealogist, she is the family historian, keeper of stories and proud of her Southern roots.

WHO SAID WHAT?

Somebody said "who is she?"
Cause we don't know where she came from
Somebody said "she's unpatriotic."
Cause she said something about American racism
Somebody said "she's an elitist"
Cause she's so damn smart.
Somebody said "she's a racist"
Cause *The New Yorker* put her on the cover holding a gun.
I saw intelligence and steadfastness
Cause I saw an Ivy League education and a symbol of African
    American completeness.
I saw beauty style and grace.
Cause I saw how women around the world admired her essence
I saw motherhood in it's finest form
Cause I saw her protect and nurture beautiful daughters
    while on the campaign trail.
Cause I saw her with "that one"
In an embrace that electrified mankind.
Now who said what?

Dera Fuller

*Dera Fuller was born in Buffalo, New York, and currently resides in
Baltimore County, Maryland. She is the program manager at a local junior
college. She is a musician, amateur writer, and artist. She is married and
the mother of two daughters.*

Dear Mrs. Michelle Obama,

Thank you so much for allowing the world and me to peep into your life during the past two years. I must say that it was a pleasure, indeed, to see what a wonderful wife, mother and daughter you are. Although we have only seen snippets of your life, it is impressive.

Candidly speaking, having stood in a similar position as a wife, mother and daughter, it is clear that you excel in these areas. It is noticeable that you are a charming, loving and intelligent woman of great integrity who knows how to set her priorities. We are so proud of you because you are a marvelous example of a classy woman. You are truly worthy of being First Lady of the United States, wife of President Barack Obama and mother of Malia and Sasha. We noticed that you are greatly adored and appreciated by them. Your family is a remarkable twenty-first-century family grounded in all the right things. My college-age grandson said to me that he would consider it quite an accomplishment to be handsome and smart. By his definition, you are quite accomplished!

My soul cried, "Yes!" as I listened to you explain to the press that you and your husband talked about this great adventure of running for the presidency, and you so wisely identified this moment as the one chance to win. My entire being agreed, wholeheartedly, with your assessment. I want you to know that I was "with" you from the announcement in Springfield and will be "with" you throughout this reign of "First Lady." I am so glad Barack got it right!

Believe me, my sister, we are going to celebrate you, Madam First Lady, the 44th President and the First Family at a presidential ball in Oklahoma on January 24. This moment in history will be celebrated by all, not as the first African American President in the world but I say, "The first on the planet in the history of the world!" I would bet that in all of the years of the planet, this has never, ever happened! I look forward to the wonderful years ahead under the leadership of an extraordinary President with the support of an extraordinary family that America will be crazy about.

Bursting with pride in Oklahoma!

Anita Arnold

Anita Arnold is Executive Director of Black Liberated Arts Center, Incorporated, in Oklahoma City. She is an author, recipient of the coveted Governor's Arts Award of Oklahoma, included in Who's Who in America, 1985, retired AT&T executive, and former member of the John F. Kennedy Center's Advisory Committee for Partners in Education.

A Tribute to Michelle LaVaughn Obama, née Robinson,
The Black Rock of Barack

FROM WHENCE SHE CAME,
DADDY'S LITTLE BLACK GAL

From The Firm Embrace of a Loving Father
Into the Heart of an African Son, Black, Beautiful,
Intelligent and Strong
Daddy's little black gal

From Mom's Little Princess
To the Most Popular Mom in the Free World,
Queen of the Country
Daddy's little black gal

From the South Side of Chi Town Protected by a Brother's Love
To Sixteen Hundred Pennsylvania Ave. NW Protected
by Secret Service
Daddy's little black gal

From Caring Daughter, Sister, Wife, and Mother
To First Lady of these United States of America
But Still, Daddy's Little Black Gal

Ina Rebecca Doss Chapman

Ina Rebecca Doss Chapman is a native of Buffalo, New York. She shares a thirty-four-year marriage and five children, Kenyatta Jameel, Mikeyta Irene, Tiffany Oria, Tera Elizabeth, and Michael, II, with the husband of her youth, Michael Chapman. They are the proud grandparents of eighteen grandchildren. Ina is an independent business woman who provides administrative and programmatic support analyzing community-based health data related to cancer.

Dear Michelle,

Awesome. Magnificent. Phenomenal.

Words too big for most women are barely large enough for you.

Woman. Daughter. Sister. Friend. Mother. Wife.

Give only a sketch of you and leave us knowing that filling in the space of who you are would take much too long.

After all, we are woman-daughter-sister-friend-mother-wife and there are meals to prepare, laundry to wash, homework to check, meetings to hold, businesses to run, husbands to kiss.

You make no apologies for the "right before touch-up" kink in your hair. Your walk applauds and pays tribute to the thickness of your thighs and the curve of your hips. Your full-lipped smile reminds us all to laugh a little more; to be happy.

Your sepia skin makes suntan lotion and skin bleaching cream ridiculous "beauty" aid caricatures. We see you and think of Hershey's candy bars; wondering why after listening to your speeches and interviews we cannot resist putting a little Nestle's Quik in our milk.

We watch you walk into a room and hear the voices of our mothers and grandmothers saying, "Stand up straight," "Hold your head up," "Look 'em in the eye when you speak."

Dear Michelle, you remind us of all that is good and right and well with us.

Now our daughters and their daughters can date young men courageous enough to secure their pants at the waist. They can feel sexy while fully dressed; leaving something to the imagination.

Honor. Compassion. Charity. Humbleness.

As we watch your rise; we dream of our own.

As we applaud you and whisper silent prayers for you and your family, we say a prayer for our becoming the women we forgot we were.

As you stand as Woman. Daughter. Sister. Friend. Mother. Wife. First Lady.
We stand with you.

We join our laughter with yours; your desires for the well-being of your children with the ones we have for our sons and daughters. We feel your joy and understand your pain because we know in our heart of hearts that you see us, feel us.

We are you. You are us.

Thank you. Thank you. Dear Michelle.

La Rhonda Crosby-Johnson lives in San Leandra, California. She is the CEO of BRUTI Enterprises in partnership with Warm spirit, Inc.

Thank you, First Lady

Thank you, Mrs. Obama for your steadfast faith; faith that the world we've hoped for can be realized. We can only surmise the emotional, spiritual and physical health that you maintained throughout your own illustrious career and that pulled you through on the dark days. Only the love and support of a community of kindred spirits, known and unknown, could have sustained you during these two years of a difficult campaign. I send you my prayers and best wishes as you begin this wonderful and blessed new chapter in your life. I know and stand proud with millions of Americans, who pray that you will succeed beyond all measure in representing our country at home and abroad.

I am a black female health executive who continues to be concerned about health care disparities and their impact on health care delivery to our communities of color. President-elect Obama's focus on health care reform is encouraging as I know that you both understand the positive and negative influence of fragmented care in our nation. Further, our patients of color must also learn to trust and be confident that they can get the care they want and deserve, as there is still distrust of the system. I am reminded of the example of my own grandmother, who lived in South Carolina. She died in her eighties, but at one point she waited until she was near death to go to the hospital for treatment for an inflamed hernia because she knew of the Tuskegee Study. As you recall this study followed black men with syphilis who were left untreated and died in the name of "good research."

I look forward to seeing your own involvement in fixing a broken system for the benefit of all of these United States. The recently passed Paul Wellstone and Pete Domenici Mental Health Parity & Addiction Equity Act of 2008 is the completion of a journey that began with Federal Mental Health Parity in 1992. I am hopeful we will not have to wait sixteen more years to witness a bill that provides health and behavioral health care equity for all citizens.

As I close, I'll ask you to remember the words of Barbara Jordan, who no doubt is smiling down from above and applauding loudly. In many of her speeches Jordan emphasized the power of love. I think that she speaks to the equity that we seek, when she said that "there may be a kingdom where the least shall be heard and considered side by side with the greatest." I quote this great woman of color as she also broke another "glass ceiling" when she was elected the first person of color to the Texas State Senate since 1883. She has always been one of my "Sheroes." She made a path for all of us aspiring to greater heights.

This year's historic electoral event gave us this opportunity to prove and realize we are a country that desires to see these possibilities each and every day.

God's Peace,

Ellen E. Grant

Ellen Grant is a native of Buffalo, New York. She was the first African American to be appointed Erie County Mental Health Commissioner. She is a community activist and serves on numerous boards and has received numerous awards and citations for her work. She is the past president of the New York State Association of Counties. She is the Vice President for Community Affairs at HealthNow of Buffalo, New York

Dear Michelle,

I was inspired to write this letter to you after attending the 26th-Annual "In the Tradition" National Black Storytelling Festival and Conference in Cincinnati, Ohio, from November 19–23. Your name, President-elect Obama and your children's names were called out often in prayer and song as we told stories around the theme: "Follow the Drinking Gourd: Celebrating Heroes and Sheroes of Freedom." Homage was paid to Rosa Parks, Sojourner Truth, John Parker, Mary McLeod Bethune, Paul Laurence Dunbar as well as the mothers, fathers, grand-parents, other family members and community persons who showed us "a way out of no way."

I know that soon your story is also one that will be told when we remember our collective stories of who we are. I envision that your story will tell of a confident African American woman from a loving family, who fulfilled the expectations of excellence in education. I want to hear a story of how you fell in love with a handsome, confident man of African descent and how together you are raising two girls with family support while pursuing demanding careers. I delight in hearing how you and Barack made a decision to seek the office of the President of the United States. The story can be told of how you faced each other and communicated to your children and family to pursue this goal and to "Keep Your Eyes on the Prize."

I am excited that many will recount this moment in history, when Michelle Robinson Obama rose from the South Side of Chicago to become the First Lady of the United States. Thank you for being an inspiration to women worldwide and from this day forward—tell your story.

Yours in sisterhood and storytelling,

Sharon Yvonne Jordan Holley

Sharon Yvonne Jordan Holley is a retired librarian from the Buffalo and Erie County Public Library. She is a member of several storytelling and community organizations and plays percussion with Daughters of Creative Sound, an African American Women's drum and percussion group. She is an "Uncrowned Queen" and believes in the power of stories to change lives. She was born in High Springs, Florida, and now resides in Buffalo, New York, with her husband, Kenneth. They are the parents of three daughters and grandparents of three grandchildren.

Dear First Lady Michelle Obama,

As an Uncrowned Queen, we celebrate you as a crowned queen. Your grace, regal carriage and dynamism as a mother, wife and role model make you a shining star in this galaxy.

You have proclaimed your primary role to be Mom-in-Chief. It is a responsibility you have performed admirably and with care and compassion. One need look no farther than Malia and Sasha to see that these young ladies radiate love. It is a direct reflection of your and Barack's caring spirit, gentle guidance and inspired parenting that they have captivated America's imagination.

You have blazed this history-making trail in a mode befitting the woman of substance that you are. As you continue this journey, be comforted in knowing that you have the admiration and respect of the world. You may encounter land mines and obstacles as you continue down this path. But, with the love of family, and with the other queens in this universe providing support, you and President Obama will conquer any challenge and emerge victorious.

Sincerely,

Barbara A. McKinzie

Barbara A. McKinzie is the twenty-seventh international president of Alpha Kappa Alpha Sorority. Her four-year term is from 2006–2010 and encompasses the organization's one-hundred-year anniversary in 2008. She is affectionately known as the "Centennial International President." McKinzie's administration is marked by the theme: ESP, which stands for Economics, Service, and Partnerships.

Dear Mrs. Obama,

Thank you for all that you have done for our country by being the living embodiment of the best in African American women. Your presence, beauty, and intelligence have had a tremendous impact on me personally. Your interest in the lives of women and in the welfare of our children makes me feel that we are connected in a very significant way. As a young mother, I focused my daily efforts on bringing up my daughter, and I can tell you that the sacrifices I made were all worth it when I look at the person she has become. The relationship you share with your husband, daughters, your mother, your brother, all of your family members and your friends, sets an example that our country needs to witness.

As chief academic officer of the Buffalo Public Schools, I am deeply concerned about the future of education in Buffalo and in our country as a whole. I am so pleased to know that you always put the education and welfare of your children at the center of your life. I urge you to focus on the well-being of our country's children, particularly those who are the most needy, by addressing the structural inequities that exist in education. I challenge you to focus on literacy, and to call together a summit of literacy leaders to address the urgent issues in our country, where one in four of our citizens are completely illiterate and one out of two are functionally illiterate. Illiteracy contributes to the large numbers of African American men who are incarcerated and unemployed. Illiteracy is at the base of the high dropout rates among African American and Hispanic males, as well as many of our youngsters who live in poverty.

I am dedicated to increasing the literacy skills of the children of Buffalo. We have an urgent need to change the culture of education in our community and our schools. I encourage you to visit our city. We need your help to make it clear to our citizens that all of our children need support to learn to read and write fluently, to think creatively, deeply and at higher levels so that they can participate in today's global society. We need your insistence that teachers receive the support they need to teach literacy skills effectively and to teach all children who come into their classrooms.

Thank you for being the gifted, responsible woman that you are. God bless you in all that you do.

Best wishes,

Folasade Oladele

Folasade Oladele is an educator with extensive experience in public school curriculum and instruction. She is currently the Associate Superintendent for Curriculum and Instruction in the Buffalo Public Schools. Dr. Oladele raised one daughter, Rachel L. Johnson, MD, PhD, who is a pediatrician and a scholar in health policy at Johns Hopkins University Hospital in Baltimore, Maryland.

DEAR MICHELLE:
REDEFINING BLACK MOTHERHOOD

At the Democratic National Convention, you introduced your husband to the audience. One of the many things you said, however, was that your daughters were the first thing you thought about in the morning and the last thing you thought about before you went to bed at night. This to me was the redefining of Black motherhood. In fact, when I think of Langston Hughes's poem "From Mother to Son," I think of the struggle that all Black mothers have had to endure for the growth and maintenance of their families. One of the messages to our children has been about struggle. Moreover, when I think about our messages to our children, I often think that we do not see Black mothers in the media except as caricatures or as superwomen; often we do not see them at all. Consequently, I believe that you will redefine Black motherhood not just for us as Black women, but as mothers.

Recently, I addressed "Mother's Day" on my blog because I had a harrowing experience as a Black mother on Mother's Day. The experience made clear to me that I was not deemed a mother, and further that that privilege was designated only for White women. However, over this past year, I have seen you redefining Black motherhood. There have been few if any national role models for such a position. In fact I would argue that you have provided for us a long-awaited opportunity to redefine Black women as *mothers*.

A hundred and fifty-seven years ago in Akron, Ohio, at a women's rights convention, Sojourner Truth declared, "Ain't I A woman?" Within her speech, Truth lamented that "I have borne thirteen children and seen em mos' all sold off into slavery, and when I cried out with a mother's grief, none but Jesus heard-and ain't I a woman?" In your words, Michelle, I feel as if you said yes! Not only am I a woman, but I claim my motherhood as one of my most important positions. I cannot think of a time when Black motherhood was considered sacred. It was not for Sojourner. She was a means of production. Her babies were born for the benefit of others. Your beautiful, gifted, intelligent daughters are your gifts. And I thank you for having them. I thank you for declaring that they are the first thing you think of in the morning, and the last thing you think of at night. It is because of our history that you can claim that concern and I can hear the words of Sojourner, my mother, and even I claim the role we value as Black women, motherhood.

In closing, I pray that your daughters, who have already benefited from the legacy of your own mother, continue to grow in the way that you envision for them, that they learn the history, the struggle and success of Black women. We are more than just mammies, jezebels, sapphires, and superwomen. I pray that they learn to define themselves as you have; as you declared to Barbara Walters that you have never defined yourself by your job. You have defined yourself by the values, love, and fortitude of the legacy passed down to you from your father and mother. I pray that this legacy will continue as you raise your daughters in your own cultural heritage defined by *Black motherhood*. Thank you for being not just the first Black First Lady, but the first Black mother.

Adah Ward Randolph

Adah Ward Randolph is Associate Professor and Program Coordinator of the Educational Research and Evaluation Program in the Department of Educational Studies at Ohio University. She is conducting research on the life of Ethel Thompson Overby, the first African American woman principal in Richmond, Virginia.

Dear Michelle,

I am absolutely thrilled that you are our First Lady and that your husband, Barack Obama, is our first Black President! I must tell you that I have never been as involved in politics as I have been this year. I made phone calls, donated money, lobbied friends and family and attended rallies. Most importantly, I stayed tuned to every phase of the campaign reported in the newspapers, on the radio and television. Whenever anything negative was reported about you or President-elect Obama, I got very upset. In fact, I've never yelled so much at the TV in my life! With my new political knowledge and my relentless vigilance, I felt qualified to defend you and Barack with total confidence that I had the truth on my side.

Even though the election is over, I intend to stay engaged one hundred percent as you have shown me how important it is to be involved in the political process. As a recent retiree from the Verizon Telephone Company, I plan to be a full-time defender of you and Barack. But that's enough about me.

I am looking at your picture on the cover of Ebony Magazine and I think you look stunning! I am glad that you are bringing your own style to the White House. I especially admire the fact that you said you are going to be "mommie-in-chief." I really admire your devotion to your children and the model of the Black family that you and Barack have elevated to a new level of respect. I have two adult children, Nicole Jeneane Seals Day and Brian Anthony Seals. Their father, Gerald Seals, and I have been married for thirty-seven years! I admire and can relate to your sense of priorities regarding your family.

In the days ahead, I know that you will be engaged in many meaningful projects. However, I know there will also be some difficult times. I want to encourage you to "hang in there" when things get rough and you have lonely moments. During those times I want you to know that I am praying for you and praying for your family's safety, everyday!

Michelle, there is another thing that I would like to share with you. Although I am thrilled about Barack's victory, I think it's sad that the color of his skin was ever an issue. However, thanks to this election we can now trace our history from slavery to the White House.

Finally, you have been compared to Jacqueline Kennedy in style. While that's a fine comparison, I think that your personal style, which you bring to the White House as our new First Lady, will be the style that many of us try to emulate. I am very proud of you, Michelle, and all the qualities you bring to your new role. Although you and Barack are the first, it's my sincere hope that you will not be the last Black couple in the White House!

Take care, because I care!

Deborah A. Seals

Deborah A. Seals is a retired Facilities Specialist of twenty-seven years for Verizon Telephone Company in Buffalo, New York. She lives in the town of Cheektowaga and has been married for thirty-seven years to husband Gerald. She is the mother of two, Nicole and Brian, and the grandmother of three. Deborah is an active member of her church.

COMETS

Michelle,

Comets only come
Once in a lifetime
And when they sail across the sky
We marvel at the beauty of the vision,
the wonder of its journey,
and its purpose in our lives.
Along its path it gains speed and grows larger and
more illustrious
and the world views it in awe.
We remember it for its brilliance and its ability to make
a difference, or a statement perhaps.
Michelle, many of us see you as our comet of the future,
and see your brightness and strength as you will soar not only
alongside your husband, and beautiful daughters
but as your own woman, mother, achiever in your own light.
Your ability to make a statement will change and impact
our lives forever.
And as you sail across our lives in the grace of motherhood,
in the harmony of family, and in the refinement of fashion,
You will collect our hearts and our support for we are
proud of you too.

Steadfast, beautiful, destined, attentive, powerful, intelligent,
determined and with a sense of self,
sprinkled with love and devotion
All the attributes of a spectacular comet,
You will make for a brilliant sight in our lives.

Michelle, best wishes to you and your family as you travel
this wondrous journey in your lives.

Sharon Renee Smith-Leonard

Sharon Renee Smith-Leonard lives in Virginia Beach, Virginia, with her husband, James, and her ten-year-old twins, Jaelan Renee and James Hayes. She is a graphic artist and teacher by profession and loves photography, writing, and traveling.

Dear Michelle Obama,

I am writing you this letter to let you know that I have been praying for you and your family and will continue to do so. We are here for a reason. We as a people have been waiting for this to take place. The White House has a Black family living there.

We all have to go through some storms and tribulations, but remember that God is there waiting for us. Just keep that in your mind while you are raising those two lovely girls. God gave them to you. As I have said before, we are here for a reason, now it is our time to show our God how much we appreciate this blessing in our time.

I have three lovely girls myself and I know there will be trials and tribulations in your life like there were, and, still are, in my life. Just keep on asking God to help you. There will be times when you feel like you don't know where to turn. Please turn to God. Love your husband and stand by him with the love of God.

I am so proud of your family for taking this path you have chosen. We have come a long way to see this day. My mother and father, sisters, aunts, uncles, nephews and grandparents are in the arms of God smiling down on you. Just know that there are a lot of us praying for and continuing to pray for you and your family.

Thanks for stepping up to the plate at this time. I know that God will continue to bless America. I thank God for you and your family for following your heart and not giving up along the way. May God bless your new home and your lives. That will be important every day. Please take care of yourself right now.

I do hope that your husband will change his mind on abortion. I look at your two beautiful girls and I just cannot see how he can let this continue to happen.

Thanks again,

Audrey Spencer

Audrey Spencer is a native of Baltimore, Maryland, and mother of three lovely daughters, Laura, Tasha, and Donna. Audrey has been a child care provider for more than thirty years and never lost a child. During that time she has cared for thousands of children. She currently volunteers in Baltimore Public Schools teaching young children reading.

MY GREAT-GREAT-GRANDMOTHER
TALKS TO MICHELLE OBAMA

Don't ever tell somebody they ain't got ta call you by your title, Baby. You humble, I know. Your beginnins is like so many women's and you wanna stay grounded and all that. Mmm-hmmm. I understand and I think that's real good a you, but I'm a tell you something: you ain't just you. Nah-uh. You alla us. You you, sure. Daughter of Fraser Robinson and Marion Shields Robinson. Harvard and Princeton graduate. And you sho' do make us right proud. But you know, you dat woman with bleedin' hands workin' double shifts in the factory, and dat Mama ain't seen her kids since the drugs got hol' of her and messed up her mind. You dat slave woman who ain't for-get her language or the river-like sound of her gramma's voice, you dat woman who jumped overboard when the bukra tried to put his hands on her. You dat big time suit wearin' sista, the happily married mother of three, you bake peach cobbler, you ordinary and you a miracle. And I know you feel funny when folk call you "First Lady" but, Baby, you best believe we been called a whole lotta something and ain't none of it had to do with high rankin' womanhood. So when they call you First Lady you think about me and all them women ain't getting a sliver of light. You turn right nice and you answer. Baby, you answer for each and every one of us 'cause for the first time in the history of this here country we gonna be called by our true name.

Sincerely,

Mariahadessa Ekere Tallie

Mariahadessa Ekere Tallie is currently learning to juggle multiple roles as a poet, writer, herbal student, wife, educator, and mother of two. She writes about art and motherhood. Her work has been published in various journals.

Dear Michelle,

A SESTINA FOR YOUR SOUL

An aura embraces your heart, your head.
You radiate; you shine
for all to see. Your life, cascading in the light
beckons millions: men, women, children: your cast
chanting and praise-dancing on center stage.
Beware the glare.

For each fleck and follicle on your head
will be scrutinized; each tear, each grimace will cast
an image on the stage—
newly curtained with strobe lights.
circling. Despite the glare,
you shine.

Inspired long before you stepped on stage,
your shine,
your place, presaged by wiser heads
who knew you would cast
a shadow of elegance beyond the spotlight,
the glaze, and glare.

Having memorized the lines, you light
the wisdom of our forebears. You shine
as you recite on this stage
of your life; while the spotlight
may glare
in your eyes, you will keep your head.

As you take a regal stand at this stage
refracting infra- and ultra-rays, you relight
a torch passed swiftly from heart to head
beyond the grumble and glare
of the dark shadows that would cast
out our light.

Your acceptance to help head
this worldwide stage
beckons millions to recast
their lives and allow the light
to stream through panes, despite the glare;
for they, too may shine.

Memory of light burns within your heart and your head,
undeterred by the sometimes harsh glare omens cast;
your vision manifests on the cosmic stage.

Dorothy Marie Rice

Dorothy Marie Rice teaches poetry and history for the Richmond, Virginia Public Schools Arts and Humanities Center. She is a wife, mother of two, and grandmother of four people. Her work has been published in various journals, including Obsidian II.

A Letter to Michelle Obama

First let me say that it gives me great pleasure to have this grand opportunity, in this extremely monumental time in American history, to tell you up close and personal, "I am so proud of you and your family."

You exude the grace, eloquence and humility that embodies all of God's beautiful creations: "WOMAN."

You've shown sheer elegance during every television show, magazine article or radio broadcast in which you've participated. You're funny, down to earth, beautiful and a woman of dignity and intellect.

I've had so many conversations with my girlfriends and we all love you. We are women from different backgrounds, who represent all colors, creeds and races. For the first time I can honestly say that I too am proud of my country. We chose the right man at the right time for the most important job in the world.

To see you and your family in the "White House" in 2009 speaks volumes. I will forever remember November 4, 2008, as it has left an indelible print in my soul. I can't even imagine how and what you must be feeling and thinking. But I know it is divine.

The road ahead will be trying, bumpy and full of surprises. However, I truly believe that God has strategically and deliberately placed us on this road as sisters together so that, together, we can overcome any barriers. I feel as though we've met in person. That's the way you make us feel. We need that feeling of connection. It's been absent for far too long, especially in the past eight years.

Michelle, I pray for you and your family every day and every night. And I thank God for answering the many prayers that brought us to this fantastic time in our history. I hold my head up even higher to know that a woman like you will be representing the "First Lady of the United States of our America" for all women. My light shines even brighter knowing the First Lady looks like me, my sister and my mother.

I look forward to January 20, 2009, when you and your family will be standing on the very steps the slaves, our ancestors, built. Oh Yes We Can, Yes We Did and Yes We Will!!

Peace love and Blessings,

Karen Bernod

Karen Bernod was born and raised in Brooklyn, New York. She is the youngest of three, raised by her mother Iris who passed in 1981. Through her love, support, and determination Karen had the opportunity to pursue her music career and to become a message through voice and song. She is a performing and recording artist as well as a background vocalist for various artists.

Dear Michelle,

STAND IN YOUR TRUTH

When the world
Wants a piece of you, a piece of him, and a piece of them
Wants all of you, all of him, all of them,
Wants none of you, none of him, none of them,

Stand in your truth
   . . . in his truth, in their truth

Remember who you are, who he is, who they are
Remember that you want him, that he wants you,
and that you both love them more than life
Remember when you have had it with yourself, had it with
    him, and had it with them

Stand in your truth
   . . . in his truth, in their truth

Root yourself
   . . . remember your roots

Ground yourself
   . . . walk on solid ground

Stand with the Creator in ALL THINGS
. . . Stand in your TRUTH

Regan Botts Ruiz

Regan Botts Ruiz is a businesswoman living in Washington, D.C. She has created a family of companies that focus on organization, attention to detail, and surrounding her clients in elegance and luxury at every level. She works to create breathtaking living and work space with her interior design firm.

Dear Michelle,

During the campaign I listened to your words closely. What stood out to me the most were your comments about how much you love your children and how much you value motherhood. There was once a time in the United States when motherhood was looked upon as an honorable institution. You have publicly brought back the respect and honor it is to be a mother.

I am also the mother of two young girls, and when you say that your children are the first thing you think about when you wake up in the morning, I know exactly how you feel. You have shown that a woman can pursue an education, work outside the home, and still keep her children as her first priority. You have also shown respect and have not underestimated the mother who works full-time inside her home. A mother affects eternity and your wonderful example as a mother will positively affect many generations to come.

I promised my three-year-old that we would have a tea party today, and she is calling right now!

Happy Mothering,

Cristi Ford Brazáo

Cristi Ford Brazáo is a wife, mother of two little girls, second-year graduate student, and a teaching assistant at the University of Utah. Some of her goals include publishing a novel, singing in the Mormon Tabernacle Choir, and teaching African American literature. She is a native of Natchez, Mississippi, and has lived in Utah for eight years.

DECISION 2008

Time did not stop
It progressed in a matter
That gave strength
That allowed wisdom to prevail
That called citizens on walkers and in
Wheelchairs
To have their say

It traveled countless miles
To the underprivileged
To the uneducated
To the ones who wanted
To get their voice back

Time did not stop
It became tangible
A handshake
A gentle touch
From a father
A man who knew
Due season needed to be now

It was created
When change became

More than hope
But a calling
A means to battle
The unspeakable

Time did not stop
But rose as shapes
Filled with blue
Showing the world that
It could be done
Old needed to see it come to pass
Young spoke
Vision instead of violence
Faith over fear
Allowed silent prayers
To become cries of acceptance
The time is now
To climb out of the valley

To walk proudly from Georgia to Alabama
From Vermont to California
For African Americans to feel
Who they always were in
A way they never thought possible
That which was last will become first
That unbelievable is now
To live it
To see it
To cherish it
Amazing Grace
Joyful tears
Uplifted spirits
The American people spoke
Textbooks will be rewritten

History was made
Forty-five years ago, a great American spoke to the masses
to not wallow in the valley of despair
to take hope for better
back to their home knowing that somehow
the situation can and will be changed

Our hearts now sing proudly the words
Thank God Almighty
We overcame

Nicole Brown

Nicole Brown is a mentor, a seventh grade English teacher at Elko Middle School, a writer, a poet, and a single mother. She started writing after personal tragedy. She shares her writing with her eight-year-old son and also with the students she mentors to encourage them to believe in themselves and work hard. She resides in Richmond, Virginia.

Dear Mrs. Obama,

Our United States of America was built by our forefathers, slaves and laborers who were forced to work or, later, had to work for little or no pay. These men and women plowed the fields, tended the crops, and raised everyone's children, both white and black. Black men and black women built this nation. How appropriate, suitable and just, now that we now also lead it.

I am proud today that I have been able to experience the most glorious and understatedly magnificent event of many generations. I remember the civil rights movement; the riots and the assassinations. I remember being bussed out of my neighborhood. In 1968, I remember initially feeling just a little uncomfortable attending my all-white, private high school. However, with all of the historic events I have witnessed in my lifetime, November 4, 2008, is undoubtedly the most magnificent.

I know that you, Mrs. Obama and your family, will have to face many sacrifices as your husband leads our nation into the unknown. But I also know that for the first time since I have been able to vote I look to the future with hope and enthusiasm. You will find it hard at times and lonely at others. But know that the weight you carry will be carried also in spirit by your sisters who understand how hard it is to be an accomplished Black woman in America. Your sisters in spirit admire and respect you and what you stand for. We will support you in the private conversations at work, in the times when things look bleak and when it seems as if no one else is there. We will support you as you take your place beside your husband. So know that there is an invisible circle of "queens" who have your back.

African American women have historically made family a priority and I admire your insistence that your daughters come first. The love, faith and devotion you display are the things I believe will get you through this exciting, yet challenging period of your life.

It is with admiration, respect and gratitude that I wish you God's speed, ultimate patience, faith and love as you travel along this road. I also wish to express my appreciation for sharing your husband with all of us who will need a strong guiding spirit in the days ahead. My three sons have followed the campaign from the beginning. The example of perseverance your husband displayed is more valuable than anything I could have told them, yet indicative of everything I tried to instill in them.

May all you wish for and pray for come true. Thank you for exhibiting the grace and confidence we, as black women, wish the world to see.

Patrice Cathey

Patrice Cathey is a resident of Buffalo, New York. She is an "Uncrowned Queen" with the Uncrowned Queens Institute for Research and Education on Women, Incorporated. Patrice is a performance poet, educator, and graduate student. She is also the Director of the Liberty Partnerships Program at Buffalo State College.

Dear Michelle,

I am so honored to be able to congratulate you on a job well done. My admiration for you is beyond words. I have two grown daughters, a sixteen-year-old granddaughter and a twenty-one-year-old grandson and I have always told my family that *can't* is not a word in our vocabulary. Now, you and President-elect Obama have made my words a reality. As a child I was taught this little saying and I passed it down to my girls:

Little drops of water, little grains of sand make a mighty ocean in the pleasant land. All that you do, do with all your might, for things done by half are never done right. (Julia Carney, 1845)

Somehow I believe you both had some of the same teaching. I am so proud of you and President-elect Obama as our leaders and as parents to your girls. You are true examples for all families regardless of race. Recently, I was in a store and a young man came in with his pants hanging down, and the proprietor told him, "Didn't you hear what Obama said, Pull up your pants!" Change is already here.

Keep Christ first in all things and he will be with you always, for no weapon formed against you shall prosper. My family and I will keep you and yours in prayer. God Bless you all.

Have a Great Day!

Evangelist Patricia Cruz

Patricia Cruz grew up in Spartanburg, South Carolina. She found a life-long career in the United States Postal Service where she worked for thirty-four years and retired as a manager of finance. She has four daughters and two grandchildren whom she loves dearly. She is an evangelist and is very active in her church and her community. She currently resides in the Bronx, New York.

A NEW GARDEN

You are unique, born of love and endowed with love.
You are a daughter, wife, mother, sister and friend.
You are bright, competent, and powerful.
You are a shaker, a reformer, a leader.
You have always made a difference
in your world, and the world around you.
You recognize and respect the unique gifts that
God has provided you and "others."
You work tirelessly to encourage and empower others
to gain strength, confidence, courage and wisdom
as you have shown.
Now as you become "The First Lady,"
caring and vulnerable because you know the truth
"to whom much is given, much is expected."
You accept this responsibility graciously as a gentle spirit,
always seeking wholeness of body, mind and spirit.
May God's blessings continue to be with you,
as you bloom in your new garden.

Lillian J. Davis-Wilson

Lillian J. Davis-Wilson is a retired Hospital and Human Service Admin-
istrator, community leader, activist, local and national Episcopal Church
leader. She is a happily married mother and grandmother. Her greatest
passions are traveling the world and engaging with people.

Dear Michelle (aka Mrs. Obama, aka First Lady of the United States of America, aka Beautiful Successful Black Woman),

I can't really think of anything profound to write. I am a simple person, so I will stick to a simple topic.

The day after the election I went to work. I work for one of the top three financial institutions in the country. I support a managing director, Mr. Bob, in fixed income. We've had regular conversations throughout the election cycle. This was the first time we spoke explicitly about race. Mr. Bob is an enthusiastic supporter of President Obama; as such he was ecstatic with the outcome of the election. As we talked about our election night activities, he made a point of saying how happy he was with the outcome and how much happier Black Americans must be.

I thought about that. Mr. Bob has an age perspective on how far Black America has come, he's in his early sixties. I'm in my early thirties. I've always expected to see a Black President during my lifetime. But I don't think I ever envisioned a Black First Lady. My reply to Mr. Bob was, "I'm glad his wife is Black. I'm glad she's not half Black, almost Black or nowhere close. I'm glad there's no confusion about her skin color or hair texture." I was surprised he understood where I was coming from. "Yeah, that's pretty awesome," he said.

Mrs. Obama, I would never presume to put the weight of a nation of women, the pain of centuries of degradation, or the sting of countless thwarted hopes for the future onto your shoulders. That's not my intent. It's not my intent to put so much on the slim shoulders of any one individual, because I have borne so many such ills from those who touch on my life. But I was amazed at how much pride I have in your existence. I was shocked to feel a sense of validation. A sense of exposure. A sense of worth in the public arena. I am a Black American Woman who now has a capable, responsible, intelligent, and faithful representative in the highest profile position in American society. You present a face, a history, a life experience of the Black American Woman that the media rarely touches on; that Hollywood occasionally uses as a sideline story for comic relief or disbelief; and that the family unit doesn't necessarily support as natural or possible.

I felt validated when your husband was elected our 44th President. Not because he's Black, but because you're Black. Don't get me wrong, this election was not about race to me. One of the things I appreciated about President Obama's campaign was his refusal to pander for the Black vote. I love the fact that his platform premise was to become President to *all* Americans. This country needs a unifier. I didn't appreciate until the conversation with Mr. Bob how much Black women needed to be validated as women outside of our communities. I immediately thought: *Black wives will be in vogue!*

Now simply speaking as a woman, as women, too, have come a long way, I say: Thank you, Mrs. Obama for being a woman of substance. Thank you for being a wife and mother. Thank you for being a well-educated career woman and solid supporter of your husband. Thank you for illustrating that our families do not have to suffer for our ambitions. It's simply a matter of partnering with the right person and walking it all out together. I admire you. Not just for the exemplary way you represent yourself, but also for your representation, support, love, affection and commitment to your man and your family.

May God continue to bless and guide you and yours.

Sincerely,

LaShawnda Jones

LaShawnda Jones lives in New York City. She works for a major financial organization.

To: The First Lady, USA
Dear Michelle, Congratulations

Greetings!

This is to let you know that we share your joy and realization of the long awaited American dream. The ascendancy of Barack to the Presidency of the United States is an achievement attained through joint efforts, and we want to congratulate you for the way you conducted yourself throughout the campaign period. It is indeed your role and character that endeared many voters to Barack's Presidency. We pray and trust that you will continue as a humble, caring and assertive mother to the people of the United States. People all over the world expect a lot from the Obama Presidency and, as the saying goes, "behind a successful man there is a successful woman." Michelle, we trust that you are equal to the task.

Congratulations!!!

Yours sincerely,

Mary Onginjo

Mary Onginjo is a resident of Maseno, Kenya with her husband, Canon Charles Onginjo and her children Dickson, Miriam, Jackline, and Robert. She is an Anglican priest and she and her husband work in the Anglican Dioceses of Maseno, South-Kismu. They serve in Maseno Parrish and she adds, we love you, we love Obama and his family for their courage and I think God has a purpose not only for the Blacks but for the whole world.

Dear First Lady Michelle Obama,

The path you are taking has long been prepared. The battered souls of our past who endured such harshness and pain never lost sight of you. Today our ancestors have awakened to a sense of great pride. And as a descendant, I too realize that the dreams they died for have come true. My First Lady, you must trust the words and knowledge, which have been given to you by your loved ones. The genuine relationship you have with your husband and your lovely daughters will serve you well.

My two daughters are about the same age as Malia and Sasha. Taylor is eleven and Madison is nine. They remind me so much of your beloved daughters. They're bright, eager learners and loving children. We have watched Sasha and Malia in the few television interviews, in which you've allowed them to participate. The girls seemed so down to earth, sweet and genuine. With all the media scrutiny that swirled around you and the President-elect, it was humbling to think that the only thing on Malia and Sasha's minds was getting that puppy. That speaks volumes about how you have grounded them. Perhaps at their young age, it's unfair to burden them with being role models, but I hope that Taylor and Madison are inspired by your daughters. In their example, I believe my girls will see how to stay humble and rooted no matter where life takes them in their pursuit of happiness.

Like my daughters, I look to you as a shining example of being grounded. You are a great model of how a woman can achieve on her own merit, support her husband's ambitions and take care of her children. I am a school teacher. While it doesn't entail the same time constraints of being a lawyer, my days are often hectic. I walk the difficult tightrope of getting my kids ready for school, getting to school myself and supporting my husband's broadcasting career. So I understand the difficulties of balancing home and work. You showed that it can be done. You were able to take care of Malia and Sasha, work and still hit the road to help your husband make history. It's not easy as you know, but I believe you will be an inspiring figure for all working moms across the country. I don't believe many former First Ladies brought that perspective to Washington.

It's so important that we, as women, are not made to feel guilty about pursuing our dreams at the same time that we provide moral and spiritual support to our family. I battle that fight all the time between friends who work and those who stay at home. I hope you use your high profile position to bridge the gap between working and stay-at-home mothers. We need to know that both choices are acceptable.

Although your path will be full of rewards there will be obstacles that you must overcome. Your belief in GOD will give you peace and direction. And your ancestral spirits will never leave your side. As you become the role model for women of the world, I urge you to hold true to your convictions and values.

God Bless,

Paulette Seals

Paulette Seals is a forty-four-year-old mother of three, who lives with her children and husband of twenty years. A Binghamton, New York, native, she now resides in Virginia Beach, Virginia. She is a kindergarten teacher assistant in the Virginia Beach Public School System.

Dear Michelle,

Wow, I feel privileged to write to you! This is a very exciting moment for me as a woman. I cried when I thought about what this really meant to me and my family as a whole to see America's first Black family in my lifetime to live in the White House. It seems like just yesterday when I finally understood what it meant to be Black in America and to know what it feels like to not be treated the same as my white counterparts. But my family always taught me to persevere, stay steadfast, and not quit, but most of all, to not let go of my dreams. There are so many women that I have looked up to in my lifetime and now I have one more to add to my count. As a mother and a new grandmother it is really important that my children and my granddaughter understand the opportunities we have and the challenges we face. It is important that they understand what it means to carry the torch for those who are unable to do it for themselves and that in each day we can and should be willing to make a difference around us. I always taught my kids to strive to be better than the last generation, by stepping it up a notch. I want them to understand that life is a gift and when one direction doesn't work out, carve another.

Because of you and your family I now know that I can still believe in the impossible. Why? Because I know in this moment and this season in time God saw fit to add to His wonderful collection of leaders a new family, one that looks like me and represents everything my ancestors said that we as a family stand for. Here is a wonderful opportunity for our country and my people to work together to make a difference in the world that we live in. That is my prayer each and every day for generations to come. I believe that you and your family can and will make a difference for the country that I live in and I am eternally grateful to God that he is allowing me to see this. I want my granddaughter to know that she can grow up and become whatever she wants to be because of those before her who paved the way. I will pray for you and your family as you move forward into your new path. For Blacks, nothing worth having has been easy, but we still find a way to make it through.

As our First Lady people can now know that there are Black women out there who have grace, style, poise and intelligence and that we can do other things besides commit crimes and destroy our lives. We have so much potential to be whatever we want to be and that is what we must hold onto. I am proud to know that you and your family represent a far greater purpose than any of us can even imagine or began to understand. Everything happens for a reason and in its season! God Bless You First Lady Obama and remember that no matter what your challenges there is someone who sits high and looks low and walks with you as you go!

Now unto Him who is able to do exceedingly and abundantly above all, we can ask or think according to the power that is in us.

Warmest regards,

Debra E. J. Thompson

Debra E. J. Thompson is a native of Buffalo, New York. She is currently the Associate Director of Instructional Services at the University at Buffalo, Educational Opportunity Center. She is the mother of an adult daughter and son and has one granddaughter.

THE CROSSINGS
(Who is prepared to hold our touch of Democracy)

Couldn't sleep last night, as I thought to myself
and remembered
scenes from China . . . just last week . . .
High Tech explosions . . . LIGHTNING EVERYWHERE
the pride, seemingly of their exhibits
of Yellow and Maroon red flags
fly'n high above the mysterious Wall
while the world lit up from Olympic beams
holding gigantic orange filled torches
hanging from every horizon within our view . . .
appearing as huge candles blowing in Asian winds
flickering amiss diverse star filled skies
and what was more apparent than ever . . . was
Technology now prevails.

Analogous thoughts prevailed this night . . . 8/25/2008
as I asked myself . . .
How important is it . . . that the flame in our country . . .
be passed on, that the torches of our past
our pessimistic thoughts mumbling's and apathies
be digitally recorded instead
that we give way

to a more enlightened generation taking over our country
when even crisscrossed computers . . . and complex
   Blackberry phones
seem to be causing us such daunting concerns.

"Hi Daddy!"
the lil' cinnamon girl
with bouncing brown curls said
while twisting with excitement
unable to stand still
certainly, unlike her sister
who was intent to stare straight ahead in amazement
as she inched closer and closer
to the technological screen displayed before her eyes
I'm sure she must have wondered
How could her Daddy . . . how could he be . . . roughly 50 ft.
   in height
How can he be so huge?
How can he be so tall?
How were all those trillions of digital dots . . . coming together
Transforming . . . transferring her Dad in such an
   electrifying style

But, my attention diverted again
to the youngest of sisters
as this lil' cinnamon child shouts out . . .
Daddy!! Hi Daddy!!
seemingly oblivious to a 75,000-person crowd
in that huge conventional hall
as she simultaneously . . . but firmly grips hands
with a tall statuesque mahogany woman
protectively standing next to her side
a deeply in-grained woman it would appear
a rich look'n woman . . . my grandmother would say

with highly polished amber shines
not a smudge anywhere to be seen . . .
and even her textures,
her colors, so to speak, were mesmerizing
I frowned a bit
as whispers of low branched weeping willows surfaced
as they began to take over my thoughts
pictures of historically untangled ropes swung back and forth
moved in the rewinds of my mind's eye.

Soon I found myself joining others on display
as tears began cascading down my face . . . as my makeup
    began to
transform
thoughts of handed down stories swirled in my mind
of the howlings . . . the howlings of the Hound dogs
the passings . . . heavy chains . . . torches in darkness . . .
    unplanned
passages
the humming of "Precious Lord . . . hold my hand . . ." thus
    recorded
thus heard
magnolia scents of stagnant brown waters . . .
and the sounds of sage green slashing waters
from indigo bodies falling within
and the air I was breathing . . .
suddenly became filled with smoldered gray smells of gun smoke
cigarette butt balconies, Kennedy's head and firings . . .
triggered by an assassin's ignorant hands
found myself sniff'n smoke . . . riots from my ole' neighborhood
12th St. Detroit
but then I smiled . . . remembering . . .
that over time . . . what's most relevant
what's most important

were those Crossings . . . those crossings towards freedom
and I knew . . . that's what I was seeing right now!

So, I'm refocusing tonight . . . 8/25/08 . . .
noting that before me . . . on my screen . . .
stands a little cinnamon child
with bouncing brown curls
and she's standing confidently and proudly
on the stage of the Democratic Convention Hall floor
Shouting . . .
Daddy . . . Daddy!!!
Where are you now??

One day . . .
but not tonight . . . surely she will really know.

*Reprinted with permission of Chickenbone Journal, www.nathanielturner.
com.*

Bev Jenai-Myers

*Bev Jenai-Myers lives in Sedona, Arizona, but is originally from Detroit,
Michigan. She retired early from the University of Michigan's Health
System's Human Resources Department. She is an author and artist. Bev is
the mother of four children and a Nana to four.*

Dear Michelle,

I have been given the unique opportunity to express my thoughts to you in the form of this letter. I will start by stating the obvious. We are all extremely proud of you and your husband, President-elect Barack Obama. We know that the success of the two of you is built on the love and respect that you have for one another.

Having been actively engaged in this historic election process, I feel a certain connection with you and your loving family. In you, I am able to see many of my own reflections; Career Woman, Mother, Daughter, Wife. All of them, approached with the importance that bears their capitalization. As Daughters, we take everything that is taught to us and mold ourselves into women who represent the good that has been bestowed upon us. As Professionals, we are able to tap into our innate sense of power. We use this power to better our communities, our workplaces, our schools, our educational institutions, our hospitals, our corporations, our churches, our nursing homes, and the list continues. We harness this power, hoping to transform the lives of all who enter our sphere of influence.

As Mothers, we find that our responsibilities are greater, yet we approach them with faith and conviction. It is specifically through this complex role that we are able to understand the meaning of unconditional love and patience. The characteristic that has become the most developed during my nine years as nurturer to four children, Stephen 9, Autumn 8, Summer 6, and Wynter 4, is PATIENCE. I am sure that your mothering experience has taught you the same. As a Wife, I have learned that the cornerstone of marriage is compassion and loyalty. It is only through compassion and an understanding of each other's life experiences that two pages come together to tell a unique story.

In closing, I began this letter with wondering what to say to you. I end this letter saying take everything with you to Pennsylvania Avenue that you have learned from the time you were an infant in a cradle on the South Side of Chicago, to your journey through the hallowed halls of Princeton University and Harvard Law. Show the world the Power, Humility, Patience, Compassion, Perseverance, and Loyalty that you undoubtedly possess. As you take your place in history as the first African American First Lady of the United States of America, do so knowing that we are with you. I am confident that you will execute your new role with grace. Your voice will be one for all the daughters across this nation and the world. The essence of your self-presentation is rooted in strong faith and prin-cipled beliefs. As you create your own legend, in the spirit of Oprah Winfrey, and the words of Pearl Cleage, "We Speak Your Name."

P.S. The arms of millions of women are connected to you and your family in spirit. Michelle, Barack, Sasha and Malia, may the grace of God be with you always.

Sisterly,

Kelly R. Beavers-Clemons

Kelly R. Beavers-Clemons is a native of Buffalo, New York. She currently resides in Atlanta, Georgia, with her husband and children where she is a practicing surgeon.

Dear Michelle,

I listened to you speak to a large crowd in Indianapolis, Indiana, on a sunny, warm spring day, April 16, 2008. As I waited outside in line with so many other excited and anxious folks, I thought—what a defining moment in my life journey. I am part of this plan to elect the first Black President of the United States.

Once seated inside, you couldn't help but feel the excitement build. Then this tall model-fine lady with strong good looks appeared and began giving her wonderful gift of words. You gave us a light-hearted reminder that we were all in this long-term dream together. And you led us to a pleasant realization that we hold the power in our hands for a better world.

There were lots of applause, vocal expressions of delight, and harmony of thoughts. People were reaching out to you and each other. Yes, we were all on this journey to the end. Your successful efforts, on behalf of your husband's campaign, have inspired us all.

My special moment with you was reaching out to take your left hand. I will always remember how we each held on with a strong grip and warm friendly handshake. I even felt your wedding rings, against my hand. I left feeling that this day would always be something very exceptional.

197

CONGRATULATIONS Michelle—our beautiful First Lady of the United States of America and hugs to your two gorgeous daughters, Sasha and Malia.

Warmest regards,

Carol L. Evans

Carol L. Evans is a seventy-year-old senior now residing in Indianapolis, Indiana, after living in Oakland, California, for thirty-six years where she was a community activist, substance abuse counselor, publisher, and fund-raiser. Since returning to her hometown of Indianapolis, she was active in the Obama Campaign as a volunteer and donor.

Dear Michelle,

Forty-eight years ago this November, a special baby girl was born. Her numerous deformities and odd shape were enough to baffle family and friends as to what to say when they saw her. Her name was Lauren Kay and she was my daughter. My heart was heavy and for a while the tears would not stop. Then one day a wise visitor came to see us in the hospital and left a card that I still cherish. On that card was written the following:

The Most Important Person . . .
on earth is a mother. She cannot claim the honor of having built Notre Dame Cathedral. She need not. She has built something more magnificent than any cathedral—a dwelling for an immortal soul, the tiny perfection of her baby's body . . . The angels have not been blessed with such a grace. They cannot share in God's creative miracle to bring new saints to Heaven. Only a human mother can. Mothers are closer to God the Creator than any other creature. God joins forces with mothers in performing this act of creation . . . What on God's good earth is more glorious than this: to be a mother?—Joseph Cardinal Mindszenty

And so, dear Michelle, continue to cherish your role as mother to your two beautiful daughters and know that this high privilege is a gift from above. My daughter died when she was two but her memory, and the gift she was, will always stay with me. Being First Mother is the most awesome role you with the help of the Creator will ever have. Enjoy and may God bless your family always.

Best wishes,

Carole Y. Finnell

Carole Y. Finnell was born in Indianapolis, and is a lifelong resident of that city. Carole worked as a professional social worker in the fields of mental health and school social work. In 2000 she retired from Indianapolis Public Schools. Carole is the mother of three sons, a daughter, and one deceased daughter. She has seven grandchildren and two great grandchildren. Her hobbies are enjoying her grandchildren, reading, traveling, and volunteering in ministries at her parish.

Dear Michelle,

You have shown us how to behave, how to talk and how to love. Your appreciation for your parents and the love that existed in your early years and throughout your adulthood has made such an impact on us. We will forever be indebted to you for this uplifting experience. It is with a made-up mind that I say to you: Be bold, Be empowered and Be blessed. What strikes me simply because it took me back to my deceased mate and love of my life is the way you and your husband look at each other. That look is so spiritual and it speaks volumes. Out of that look came your two lovely and precious daughters. I shall do all in my power to advance the cause of peace and justice and love, which is so evident in your persona.

I shall study to gain knowledge for in knowledge there is power. Your brilliance is so inspiring and as a Clinical Social Worker / counselor for teens, I have begun to teach them the importance of seeking excellence in everything they do so that their goals can be limitless. You are a wonderful role model. In the words of Alicia Keys you are a superwoman. The ancestors are singing their songs and smiling.

Thank you Michelle, God bless.

Allie H. Freeman

JOYFUL TO MICHELLE

Spirit filled, joyful to the vessel of womanhood
Carrying the torch is understood, First Lady
We will be there for you joyful
Brilliance a plenty, joyful
Pride in your presence, grace and mercy, joyful
Caring and family solidarity, joyful
Prayerful and thankful as you transcend
Wife and mother, proud of your kin
Joyful to you.
May the Creator protect and guide
We stand by your side
Joyful women, who are many in this place and in this land.

Allie Freeman is a seventy-four-year-old clinical social worker, practicing in a high school. Her hobbies are dancing, writing and reading. She delights in her three sons, daughters-in-law, and six grandchildren. She lives in Buffalo, New York.

Dear Michelle,

Three words sum up this miraculous event—Look at God! Congratulations on being the first African American First Lady to occupy the White House, as wife of the first African American President, Barack Obama. I am so very proud of you both. Like you, for the first time I am now proud to be an American. As wife, mother of two precocious, beautiful little girls, and career woman, you set the standard for all females to aspire toward, regardless of race. Your elegance and strength are admirable as well as your views on issues that matter to us as Americans, generally, and as African Americans, particularly. Your husband is not only wise but also a visionary, and your attributes of superior knowledge and rare beauty provide for him the perfect complement.

So far, you, Barack and your mother have managed to keep your daughters grounded, and that is commendable. I can imagine that maintaining their privacy will be somewhat difficult, especially with the press and the paparazzi constantly at your heels attempting to make news out of events that are not newsworthy. But I have every confidence that you will do everything humanly possible to continue to rear them in a normal fashion despite the extraordinarily public life that you will be leading. Also, I am glad that they will have their Daddy, and you will have your husband, at home most of the time.

You and Barack epitomize the strong Black family who must juggle jobs, children, and organizational responsibilities. Moreover, you exude a self-assuredness and confidence borne out of strong family values based on belief in God. Your dedication to your fellow humans, particularly those who are less fortunate, is commendable. Thank you for being the dedicated, community-minded individuals that you have been, even when you were not in the limelight, and for continuing these actions. I have been praying for the safety of your husband and your entire family ever since his candidacy. Just know that I will continue to pray that God will surround all of you with a "hedge of protection."

I know that you and Barack are not Southern, and I am not sure whether you like pecan pie; nevertheless, I thought that you might enjoy this dessert. It is always a hit wherever I take it for large gatherings, particularly at Thanksgiving and Christmas dinners. At the extended family Thanksgiving dinner, this pie plate was the first to be "cleaned," all slices disappearing within a matter of minutes. It has a surprisingly light and fluffy texture that is sure to please palates and waistlines.

You and Barack helped us, as African Americans, to audaciously hope for a dream that has come true. We thank you, we love you, and we support your efforts to make America and the world better places in which to live.

Blessings,

Shirley A. James Hanshaw

PECAN PIE

Press 'N Bake Cream Cheese Crust

1 pkg (3 oz) Philadelphia cream cheese at room temperature

½ cup (1 stick) butter or margarine, softened

1 cup sifted Martha White all-purpose flour

Combine cream cheese and butter; blend well. Stir in flour. Refrigerate about 1 hour. Remove dough from refrigerator and press into bottom and up sides of 9-in pie plate (that has been sprayed with Baker's Joy or Pam cooking spray).

Filling

4 eggs, lightly beaten

1 cup sugar

1 cup light corn syrup

½ cup (1 stick) butter or margarine, melted

1 teaspoon (each) vanilla & lemon flavoring (decrease or increase according to taste)

1 cup pecan halves (more if you prefer)

1 unbaked Press 'N Bake Cream Cheese Crust (above)

1 tablespoon bourbon (secret ingredient)*

Preheat oven to 350 deg F. Combine eggs, sugar, corn syrup, butter and flavoring(s) in large bowl; blend well. Stir in pecans. Pour into prepared crust. Bake 45 to 50 minutes or until set, covering outer edges with foil to prevent over-browning, if necessary. Cool on wire rack.

*NOTE: If you are a teetotaler, you can omit this ingredient; however, it does add a certain *je ne sais quoi* to the taste. It also makes the filling "light," and, besides, it evaporates during the cooking process.

Shirley A. James Hanshaw lives in Mississippi and teacher at Mississippi State University. She is the author of several books and is currently completing a new book on Vietnam and African Americans in that war.

Dear Mrs. Obama,

I was born fifty-three years ago in the South, in the midst of racial unrest related to voter registration and civil rights. Like Langston Hughes, I've known rivers, deep, dark and dusky but they have brought me and you to this place of triumph and victory. As a child growing up in Haywood County, Tennessee, site of the 1960–1961 Tent City when African Americans were driven from their homes because they registered to vote, my mother poignantly shared her struggles for the opportunity to vote. She, along with her neighbors and friends, stood in the sun for days during 1959–1960 until they were able to register. Many of them proudly voted for the first time in the 1960 election.

Though she was more than forty years old then, every election day has been precious to us. One of the last things she did this year at eighty-nine years old was to escape the clutches of Alzheimer's disease long enough to know that she had voted for her first African American President. The lonely tear that trickled down her beautiful face on November 4 after she knew the election's outcome was the culmination of her hopes and dreams, long deferred but never forgotten. We knew this day would come but could hardly believe that it had happened in our lifetime.

You and your beautiful family are what we have yearned for! You are hope, light, promise—flesh and blood that says yes,

African American women can be proud, gentle, graceful and grace filled, intelligent, strong but compassionately positive role models. A force to be reckoned with! You show that we can love our husbands and children because we have had parents who loved each other and us. I fully understand that helping you and President Obama move our country and world to a more just place will take all of us striving for the best from ourselves and our neighbors. We must hold each other and hold each other accountable for our choices, we must speak truth in love, we must accept no limitations or excuses from ourselves or our government and together we can and will stand tall.

My prayer is first, when you are tired, you will listen to your heart and rest and renew yourself; second, when you don't please everyone, you will understand the futility of even trying and you will trust the scriptures and lean not to your own understanding, but trust the author and finisher of your faith with all that concerns you; third, you and your family will let us help you make the world better because "many hands make light work"—it's what my mom always said and she's always right!—and finally, fourth, that you will soar with the eagles and take us with you! Be blessed as you shine brightly and lead the way.

Yours in the pursuit of Excellence,

Cynthia A. Bond Hopson

Cynthia A. Bond Hopson lives in Lebanon, Tennessee. She is a motivational speaker and the author of four books. She is the Assistant General Secretary for the United Methodist Church, Black College Fund. She and her husband, Roger, a United Methodist minister, have two children and four grandchildren.

Dear First Lady Michelle Obama,

Thank you for just being who you are and for using the skills that God has graced you with to remain a strong woman dedicated to family and the betterment of this country. You are a source of inspiration to me and have been for years. As a law student, I have followed your career and the decisions you made to maintain a balance in your family, marriage, career and community service. My mother is from the South Side of Chicago. My father is deceased. I know that my father is so pleased with what I have done so far in my life. I am sure yours continues to be an angel watching over you. I pray that strength, grace, courage, and peace remain in your life, especially during the next four years. As the official host of this country, I know that you will represent the United States of America in a way that will change the role of First Lady and all that she can accomplish.

During the presidential election, you maintained a posture of confidence, support for your husband and a belief that change can happen. I felt so relieved and blessed that this change was realized on November 4, 2008. I am so proud that you, President Obama, Sasha and Malia will make the White House your home. My career choice as a child was to become the President of the United States and whenever I was questioned about becoming the first African American President, I always replied that I hoped I would not be the first. If that position is still a possibility in twenty years, I hope to be the third African American President and the second woman, after you.

Grace, peace, mercy and protection to your family as you continue to do what you have been called to do.

Sincerely,

Candacé McGill Jackson

Candacé McGill Jackson is a native of Virginia. She is a third-year law student at the University at Buffalo Law School. Currently she serves as the Graduate Assistant in the Center for Academic Development Tutorial Lab, a University at Buffalo Law Student Ambassador, and as a member of the Student Bar Association Board of Directors.

Dear Michelle,

This letter is written in memory of Queen Hatshepsut, Maria W. Stewart, Harriet Tubman, Ida B. Wells, Hattie W. Spears, Ida M. Johnson, Annie M. Johnson, Sandra M. Reddick, and Charshee McIntyre.

Congratulations on becoming the 46th First Lady of the United States and the 2nd First Lady of the 21st Century. It is an honor to write a letter of hope, encouragement, and inspiration. In the past, most of the First Ladies have stood behind their man. In the two years of campaigning, you stood beside your President-elect Obama. Throughout the campaign, there wasn't a time that your name wasn't mentioned. As the campaign progressed and you began to emerge, it gave me greater respect and understanding of President-elect Obama. In his speeches, I can see where his inner strength lies.

Going back through the annals of African American history, the vision of the past has come to light. The day has come that we are able to look at ourselves and the First Family of the United States with respect, great intelligence and without fear. The past two years have shown the strength of the African American woman, and how she's able to manage a career, a family and still work in the community. African American women will have to show our support of your plans for the future.

When Maria W. Stewart lectured before her audiences, she told women to look deep inside of them, find their talents and use them to the best of their ability. We have seen your ability to lead, to motivate, and encourage others just as Mrs. Stewart did in the 1830's. Harriet Tubman would say, "If you're tired, Keep Going; If you're scared; Keep Going, If you're hungry, Keep Going; If you want to taste Freedom, Keep Going."

Michelle, I say to you, if you get tired; keep going, we'll be there to help you through. If you get scared, keep going, we'll be there to build you up. If you get hungry, keep going, we'll be there to feed you, and strengthen you. And if you want to taste freedom, keep going because you already have.

Remember, your ancestors are always with you. They will continue to be your guide and your strength. Never be afraid to reach out and ask your ancestors and your sisters for help.

Love you and your family, keep up the good work.

Debra M. Johnson

Debra M. Johnson is a member of the Harriet Tubman Retreat / Memorial Library Project. Debra Johnson was born in Buffalo, New York. She is the mother of one son. Currently Debra is a student at Canisius College. She has been involved with study groups, block clubs, and various community organizations.

Dearest Michelle,

Congratulations on such an awesome achievement for your entire family. It goes without saying that this past election sea son has energized the national electorate in a manner that is unparalleled. I have not been alone in my increased enthusiasm for the democratic process, but what has felt singular is the magnitude with which I have identified with *you*, as the first representation of ME in your role as "First Lady" of the United States. Never before have I contemplated the complexity of the daily struggles of the person who is the President's biggest supporter and confidant. What an awesome responsibility.

As a little Black girl from the South Side of Chicago, with an Ivy League degree and a strong sense of self and family, I have always received the message that I am supposed to be certain things. External expectations have been imposed at every turn. No matter what I've done or thought, I am described with many labels: too strong, too confident, too intimidating to men, my success means the failure of others, I'm angry, I'm loud, I'm a know-it-all and I'm a superwoman. The list is long and expressed in many subtle, but mostly overt ways. I have only been allowed to be a caricature, symbolic of the lack of collective worth this country has had for Black women. I'd become numb to, and had all but accepted, this as the hand I'd been dealt.

213

And then you came along. This stunning, striking, funny, down to earth, fly, Black girl from the South Side of Chicago, with an Ivy League degree. As I began to get used to seeing your face on the television these past months, I realized one day, I am Michelle, Michelle is me! It was at first a light-hearted proclamation between my girlfriends and I, but as the reality of your husband's imminent victory sank in, it became a sort of mantra, a new badge of honor. For the first time, I was afraid, not for your husband, but for YOU. Not a fear for your safety, but for your freedom. The question I kept asking myself over and over again was *Who do YOU get to be? Who do YOU get to be?* I asked this question as I looked at *myself* in the mirror, and for the first time, I didn't have any idea what the answer was *supposed* to be.

It is truly limitless, and shapeless, and unprecedented. You (and I) are everything, you (and I) are whatever you want to be, you (and I) are nothing that has ever been seen before. How freeing! How terrifying! I keep trying to express to my boyfriend what this moment means to me, and he just doesn't get it! For the first time in my life, not knowing the answer is a good thing! This is uncharted territory and I am glad to be taking the first steps with you. No expectations, just a new journey. Thank you for your courage. Thank you for your authenticity. Thank you for your love.

So as you begin your tenure as *my* first, First Lady, go freely, and without burden or expectation. You can do no wrong because you ARE the mold. Congratulations.

Your kindred spirit,

Amanda Williams

Amanda Williams was born in Chicago and grew up on the South Side where she attended the University of Chicago Laboratory Schools. She is an artist and architect and she uses her work to explore themes of personal freedom and identity. She has exhibited extensively throughout the United States, including the Studio Museum in Harlem and numerous other venues.

Dear Michelle,

Thank you for raising the bar for Black women everywhere.
You are an example of what is possible with loving and supportive parents, focused determination, vision and choices
which honor oneself and one's dreams. Even those of us who
didn't have the benefit of such great parents are inspired to
build upon whatever foundation we have. We all see how
important it is to provide a solid foundation of love and support for our children.

You show us that we can be family oriented *and* have a
successful career, doing work that makes a difference. You
and your family are always so genuine. It's a testament
to your parenting that your daughters are so well adjusted
that this whole experience barely fazes them. Case in point:
When Sasha saw her Daddy on the screen at the Democratic
National Convention, she grabbed for the microphone and
talked to him as though they were on a videophone. She
seemed oblivious to the fact that there was an audience of
tens of thousands in the room and tens of millions watching
via television. You couldn't have asked for better kids to travel
with you and Barack on this journey.

You provide us an example to marry an equal who recognizes us as an equal. You chose a man with maturity, compassion and vision. He not only has potential, but is actively living

out his potential. He is a man who sees his responsibility as a father and an equal parent to his children—a whole parent, fully participating in his children's lives. It's beautiful to see some of your moments together. It's like there's only the two of you. You exude so much genuine love and respect that it's visible. It is so evident. I had never seen that kind of absolutely authentic, not-for-public-consumption kind of connection between a high profile couple before. The world goes away, and it's just the two of you, knowing all you've been through leading up to those moments. So natural and effortless, you flow together, and that is powerful for us to see. He melts into you in such a way that I could *see* that you are his rock before he ever uttered those words in Grant Park. So many Black women are the rock of the family—your husband acknowledges and appreciates that.

Your example has touched my heart so much. It has reminded me, and hopefully all Black women, to cherish our values enough to live the life of our dreams and choose a partner who truly loves, adores, and respects us and with whom we can travel life's journey as equals and complements.

Millions of Black women worldwide now see what is possible, if we surround ourselves with love and support, honor our gifts and dreams and choose a partner wisely.

Thank you and God bless you,

Attica Georges

Attica Georges lives in Oakland, California, and is cofounder of Circle of Sisters, a women's group in her hometown of Oakland, where she is a socially and politically engaged community member. Attica enjoys learning new things, meeting new people, questioning conventional wisdom, discussing ideas, and traveling the world.

Dear First Lady Michelle Obama,

I thank God for blessing us with an amazing, strong African American woman who inspires and motivates, and has opened the door for African American women to enter. All of us have had our lives changed by the visual of your presence. You have moved the ball forward on the image of African American women and on how the world sees us and how we see ourselves. You are the epitome of strength, endurance, perseverance, faith and love and I thank you for making me realize the power that I hold as an African American woman. You have given hope to our daughters, that with hard work and study they may elevate themselves to aspire to whatever they want to become. Your role is far greater than you will ever know and, using the words of Dr. Maya Angelou, you truly are the ultimate "Phenomenal Woman." May God continue to bless and protect you, President Obama, Malia, Sasha, your mother and your entire family.

President Barack Obama and First Lady Michelle Obama. How sweet the sound!

Sincerely,

Barbara Glover

Barbara Glover lives in Buffalo, New York. She is the owner of Miss Barbara's School of Dance, which has been operating for nearly forty years. Many of her students have achieved recognition throughout the country.   217

MICHELLE OBAMA

Her spirit is so strong
yet gentle enough
to love
to laugh
to lead
to be the rock that Barack needs

She is sweet
and compassionate
in a way that is genuine
and so loving
Our First Lady embodies grace

She is renaissance!

Finally someone
who meets the definition of a strong woman
she's the one we look up to
and aspire to be
at this moment in time
She has been called to embrace our nation

Cornelia Yvette McCowan

Cornelia Yvette McCowan is a higher education administrator. She has spent the last ten years inspiring and empowering young people to make their dreams a reality. She lives in Lancaster, Texas, with her two children, Daniel and Taylor.

Dear Michelle,

I wanted to first say thank you for being the woman, the daughter, the wife, the mother and soon to be First Lady that you have been, are and are becoming. You have allowed me without any doubt to feel proud to be an educated, African American woman, mother of four girls and wife. Living the life of an ordinary woman from Brooklyn, working hard trying to be of service to others counts for something. My vote made a difference. Finally a President who speaks for those of us lost in the middle of the haves and those who have lost hope. For the first time in my life time I have a President and a First Lady who walk their lives in faith. They recognize and know the plight of the masses in this country. I can't tell you how miraculous a thing that is for me and many others. I don't even think many can put into words what it is that attracts them to you and Barack's side. Just that there is an innate attraction to that which is true, honest and good. Yes our country is in a poor state of affairs. We needed change, but a change that didn't require a color label, a religious label, or class label. It had to be a spirit that carried hope from an insatiable supply of unyielding grace, acceptance and forgiveness to set the tone and intervene for this election's victory. A spirit of healing had to be omnipotent. The synchronicity of the world's events, opponents, war, the present Commander-in-Chief and financial crisis played its part. But no one man could change the tide of a country without a higher force being within him and the woman at his side. I know in my own life when I have strayed from my relationship with God, I have left myself at a disadvantage in the world. So as I and many more will be praying for your constant faith and success in what you do, don't loose sight of God. We have "come this far by faith."

In God We Trust,

Cynthia Robinson-Bioh

Cynthia Robinson-Bioh resides in Brooklyn, New York. She is a forty-six-year-old African American of both Native American and Scottish descent. She is an educator by profession and a writer by passion. She is a wife and mother of four girls.

Dear Mrs. Obama,

2008 is a Very Good Year. It's a very good year for octogenarians like my husband and I, from the Buffalo, New York area, who never thought we'd live to see an African American in the White House. Now we pray that you and Mr. Obama can weather the tsunamis about to wash upon your shores.

We ask that you remain faithful to your beliefs and values, which have taken you far despite the obstacles placed in your path. Beware the beguiling Siren's Songs that will entice you to stray. Be vigilant, careful and strong. African Americans salute you from near and far, people in lands across the seas look forward to your governance. We have faith that you will not betray us.

Hugs, Love and Prayers,

Georgia Mackie Burnette

Georgia Mackie Burnette a native of Buffalo, New York, enjoyed a career in nursing as Assistant Professor of Nursing, Niagara University and Director of Nursing, Roswell Park Cancer Institute. She is now a freelance writer addressing issues in health care, travel, family reunions, and local Black history.

Congratulations to the First Lady of the United States,
Michelle R. Obama,

What an amazing accomplishment for you and your family! I am sure that the journey was long and hard. However,
from everything that I have heard you say and read about your
journey, I am sure that your father would be very proud. You
showed us what he showed you; never give up, fight through
your challenges and in the end you are a winner. I am equally
sure that your mother is a big factor in shaping who you have
become. My mother is in my life as well. When I see your
mother with you and your family it harkens back to the days
of old when Black families were a close group that supported
each other in whatever endeavor we set out to do.

I see this election as a way to reclaim that which has been
missing in America, especially Black America—family. First,
family is to be honored and second, family really does matter.
You have carried yourself with confidence, grace and elegance.
Those attributes are equaled by your intelligence. Your decision
to have Christ in your life has not been hidden under the bushel
and is a testament to your faith. For that, I sincerely "THANK
YOU." I am not sure that anyone seeks to become a role model
for a nation, but inevitably it is not always a chosen destiny. I
believe that your husband has been called to the kingdom for
such a time as this and as his helpmate, so have you.

Since 1968 Black America, in my opinion, has taken a downward turn in our familial relationships. We have been wandering around in the wilderness for 40 years. Since this election many people, both men and women, have been prompted to take a look at themselves and ask "how do I get myself together?" I think this behavior is the result of what they have seen the Obama family portray. That is a good thing for Black America and America as a whole. For that we say "THANK YOU."

On a sisterly level, I have spoken with our senior women, middle-aged women and young women coming of age. One thing they have all said, "What an inspiration she is." Inspiring in the sense that it is okay to be a strong woman, an educated woman, a mother and a wife—one who loves her husband and is not afraid to exhibit all these attributes; even in public. We don't see you as someone who is trying to prove herself but as a lady, who is self-confident. She can support her husband and still stand on her own. Again, we say "THANK YOU!" That example has been missing for such a long time.

The days will be long, the highs will be high and the lows will be low, but rest assured as long as the Obama family keeps their hands in God's hands you will never walk alone. A three-fold cord is not easily broken. A final "THANK YOU" for showing us and sharing with us your story and your family. May your angels protect you and the grace and blessings of the Lord forever give you peace.

Your Sister In Christ,

SaBrina Francesca Brown

SaBrina Francesca Brown is a fifty-year-old single Black female residing in North Beach, Maryland. She feels thankful and blessed to have her mother and her grandparents living. She has one brother who has passed; however, her profile would not be complete without him. Moreover, these are the people who have helped to shape the woman that she has become.

AN ODE TO FIRST LADY
MRS. MICHELLE OBAMA

The Westchester County Club of the National Association of Negro Business and Professional Women's Clubs Inc. is exceedingly proud to join hands with the global community to share in the greatest historic celebration in our time, your becoming the First Lady of the United States of America, the first African American to hold the prestigious position.

Mrs. Obama, superior intellect, vision, hope and determination are your virtues. It is inevitable that you will rise so graciously to the occasion. We are just so thrilled that the time has come for the African American community to shout for joy for having his honor, President-elect Barack Obama, become the 44th President of the United States of America. Words are inadequate to express the mood of the people all over the world.

Everyone welcomes change; it came at the appointed time. There is so much in the offing that generates faith, hope and charity that will inspire one to move forward with convenient speed for a better tomorrow. On November 4, 2008, the people spoke, the inauguration of the time for change became history. Peoples in the four corners of the universe shared one common accord, "Its Time for a Change."

Mrs. Obama, you are such a Blessing! We celebrate you. You have so much to offer. You are a rare find, a source of great

227

pride. Your modus operandi is geared for excellence. You think critically, reason analytically, and communicate effectively to cross the bridge to the 21st Century. Mrs. Obama, because of your sterling worth, women of all ethnic backgrounds and persuasions are inspired by the manner in which you present yourself; so elegant, so graceful and charming. They have already put it to practice. Everyone is feeling a sense of inner pride just for your being who you are, Michelle Obama, First Lady of the United States of America. You are revered all over the world by millions because of your captivating personality.

Mrs. Obama, with all the excitement and continuous celebration, it is almost unbelievable that an African American has been elected President of the United States of America during our lifetime. The Reverend Dr. Martin Luther King, Jr., articulated it well when he said: "Do not judge me by the color of my skin, but by the content of my character." Surely, from a historical perspective, President-elect Barack Obama is the revelation of Dr. King's dream. In the interest of justice, the time for change came at the appointed time. Mrs. Obama, glory is to God. You have reached the pinnacle of success; blessed with a well-appointed First Family, the wife of the President of the United States of America; mother of two beautiful first daughters, the daughter of a very loving and protective First Grandmother of the United States of America, residing as First Family in the White House, which is so well appointed for gracious living in the nation's capital, Washington, D.C.

Mrs. Obama, the members of the Westchester County Club of the National Association of Negro Business and Professional Women's Clubs Inc. wish you a multitude of blessings, and continued success in abundant measure in the years to come.

Respectfully,

Beryl Small

Beryl Small is president of the Westchester County Club of the National Association of Negro Business and Professional Women's Clubs, Incorporated. The club celebrated its 55th Annual Founders Day Celebration in 2008. Members of the Westchester County Club of NANPBW continue to extend themselves throughout the community in civic, social, and educational work.

Michelle

WHEN WE HEARD THE NEWS

Girl we all hollered
We danced in the streets
We drank good wine
we all threw our hands up in the air
Towards the sky
we all shouted
Hallelujah, Hallelujah
Let gods work be done
The time has come
And sister we are ready

We are all sisters moving and swinging all over the place
we all are doctors and teachers and lawyers and singers
dancers and piano players, we all harmonize together
Hallelujah, Hallelujah
We are skaters and bicycle riders and truck drivers and given'
    Parties for the babies and the teenagers and Uncle Joe and
Aunt Mae

We all are sisters
After riding the freedom buses
Back and forth to Washington

After being put in jail for
Protesting in front of the United States Department of
    Agriculture
Holding signs up for the government to give families food
    stamps
Taking busses to Washington again to try and stop the war
    in Vietnam
Standing and protesting in front of the White House
After sending Congress one zillion letters of protest
After fighting for women's rights in the Women's Studies
    department
At all the universities all across the land
After riding buses back and forth to
Albany protesting the cuts in education for minorities and
    women
And my sistergirl Dorchell stood up and
spoke for the masses
she was even written up the Albany newspaper
She was standing up and speaking up
After visiting Sparta Georgia located in Hancock County in the
summer of 1959
Trying to buy an ice cream cone and receiving the
Comment back from across the counter. We don't serve
    niggers here
After all the standing and sitting and the letter writing and
    the telephoning and
meetings with our sisters
Who never once gave up day after day and week after week
    after week and night after night
And year after year
Gathering together to discuss the issues at hand
Fighting for our lives
All us sisters

We travel by land, sea and air

Sisters all over the place
Even my white sister friends called to say they were elated
I told them so am I

I shouted for myself as loud as I could scream
I shouted again for my daughter
Tolley who recently received her PhD from TSU
And not without a struggle
You feel me

I shouted you hear me
I screamed
At last a black beautiful woman is in the White House
And we shouted some more for ourselves
and for our mothers and for our mother's mother and for
our sisters
we all screamed and we hollered and we jumped up and down
Michelle Obama it is indeed one of my greatest pleasures to
have you in the White House
The work has not been in vain
God Bless America

We hollered
We all screamed
We dropped our telephones
We danced in our houses and in the streets
We threw our hands up in the air and shouted Hallelujah,
Hallelujah
We cried
We sisters celebrated you
MICHELLE OBAMA, We celebrated you . . .

Shirley Sarmiento

Shirley Sarmiento was born in Buffalo, New York. She is an educator/poet/ producer/social Activist, writer, and lecturer. She is currently writing a book with her daughter soon to be available. Shirley has worked and volunteered for many community agencies in Buffalo.

Dear Michelle,

You look wonderfully fierce in red. On you, red is magical and transformative. Red is also the color of an evolved warrior such as Shango, guardian of the sky. Indeed you are the keeper of your family's crown, making sure your soul mate, and our President, Obama's head is anchored in the heart, yet rooted to the ground.

As the Black woman/sister that you are, you set the bar for all of us, showing the world what we have always known: talent, intellect, common sense and grace reside in you, in all of us, revealed in the way you carry yourself. I love what I have seen in you so far! You know and love yourself and will not allow anyone to dictate what you should look or sound like. You insist on naming your specific African American experience without being muffled. Through your alluring manner and tactful disposition the world will come to know all of us and the various paths that we have walked to be present in this moment.

As a mother of three young adult African American children, I am grateful to be a witness at this decisive moment in history. The night of the election victory my seventeen-year-old daughter, Teju, and I hollered and cried at the Democratic Convention Center in Oakland, and had our own pow-wow via telephone with my other two children, Shola in New York and Jawara in southern California.

Family is also sacred to you. Almost everything that I have heard you and President Obama say confirms that this will be your greatest challenge, to continue to rear your girls in a manner that is in keeping with your core values under such public scrutiny. Continue to love and guide them fiercely, but also be flexible. Laugh a lot and forgive easily. Allow Malia and Sasha to be princesses. They choose to be daughters of a President so allow them to bask in the attention and pampering that they have earned. Luxury and ease do not make a person mindless, but rather lack of direction about responsibility. The way you live your life as the First Lady and the way Obama manages this country as President will serve as the blueprint for your girls. I rejoice and welcome these First Girls of the White House.

Michelle, take care of you. Continue to keep your sister-friends close. Listen to all, but only accept the counsel of a trusted few, who you know have your and the country's interest at heart. Be the sounding board for President Obama. He needs you now more than ever to stay grounded and remain steadfast in his integrity and commitment to create an America that works for the majority of Americans, an America where transparency rules. You are so aptly placed. I have full confidence in you.

Do not be afraid to discover and share the evolving Michelle that must step forth into this glorious new dawn. In African cosmology, the one who tends to the head is the most important person. President Obama is the head of the nation. However, you my dear, as mother of future leaders, as wife of the most powerful man in the world, your role as custodian of their minds is pivotal and essential to the harmonizing balance that will be brought to the world. Michelle, like so many powerful women in history from Harriet Tubman to Fannie Lou Hamer and Queens Nzinga and Hatshepsut, your consciousness, clarity and love will help to ensure that the world rotates at an even, gentle pace. So be powerful and be the ultimate, chic, African-American warrior First Lady.

Pride and joy color my heart to see you installed. You and your family have been and will continue to be lifted and protected by my prayers. I exult at your unfolding.

Opal Palmer Adisa

Opal Palmer Adisa is a resident of Berkeley, California. She is a professor of graduate writing and literature at California College of Art. Africa blew breath into me, Jamaica baked me and America nudged my growth, and as such I belong to all and yet only to myself. I am a woman as soft as the translucent clouds and as sturdy as fibrous yams. I am daughter and mother, friend and sister, lover and confidante. I write in and out of the meaning of love to find the truth alive in the dream.

Dear Michelle,

Open the Closet Door on Mental Illness

As an African American, female psychiatrist I am confronted daily with the ravages of mental illness on individuals, families and communities. The major problem that confronts treating mental illness is the denial and hostility toward mental health care. People are intensely fearful of mental illness. In my own family my mother had a serious mental illness and died in a mental institution, yet many in my family refuse to admit she had mental health problems. As a nation, we continue to hide impaired family members in the basement, attic and closet. It is time to *Open the Closet Door on Mental Illness,* and replace myth and fiction with facts.

As a child I remember walking home from school with three friends. As we walked down Stanton Street we saw this woman walking toward us; she was disheveled, disoriented and limping along. My friends started to laugh and point saying, "Look at that lady, she looks crazy." I looked at the lady. It was my mother.

My heart started pounding and my hands trembled. I felt dizzy and faint and I wanted to melt into the ground. I wanted to talk. I started to talk, but my mouth was unable to open. My tongue felt glued to the palate. My mind was screaming, "That's my mother! Don't laugh at her!" But the words never came.

She limped down the road unaware that her daughter had not owned her. I became angry at myself and my friends. Who were these girls for whom I sacrificed my mother? They did not really care for me, while I know my mother loved me and had protected me many times from abuse. I was ashamed because she was mentally ill and I did not understand that this was not anyone's fault, neither hers nor mine.

This illness caused great pain for her and her family. The available treatment modalities in those days were not as extensive as today and the needed support services were not in place. My mother spent many years in a mental institution, often was in a straitjacket, and was thus not able to guide or see her children grow up and develop. Her absence from the family was very disturbing and resulted in multiple family dysfunctions. She died an early death while institutionalized.

Why would a child have to try to figure all this out? Family education about mental illness is critical and could save families the heartache we experienced growing up. The country desperately needs a better system of care for the mentally ill and the mentally disadvantaged.

So Dear Michelle, help to *Open the Door on Mental Illness*.

Love and Congrats,

Dr. Curly

Curlane Jones-Brown, affectionately known as "Dr. Curly," lives in Buffalo, New York. She is a practicing psychiatrist and an author of several books. She has devoted her career to the facilitation and maximizing of individual potential. She is the devoted wife of Dr. Lloyd Brown and the mother of five.

Dear Mrs. Obama,

I am pleased to have this opportunity to congratulate you and President-elect Barack Obama on a successful campaign. America is proud you! It was the most dignified and impressive campaign I have ever seen. Words cannot express the depth of my feelings of joy and the tears shed as the election results ensured that your husband would be our next President. I wish both of you much luck and success as you make your journey to the White House and begin a new historic era.

You have made such a great impression on the world and have become a role model to many women. President-elect Obama's and your vision to change America has inspired so many young men and women to become more involved in efforts that impact the world. This history-making election, while inspiring some, has reinforced the hope and faith of black men and women in a manner that is, perhaps, greater than you can imagine.

As a seven-year-old child I dreamed of becoming a nurse. I was inspired by an illness that forced me to spend nine months in a hospital on a pediatric unit. While many thought my dreams were much too high, I never stopped dreaming and through prayer, I kept the faith. My lengthy hospitalization, at such a young age, was a defining experience that turned a dream into a reality. Today, I am a nurse and I am a nurse educator. I am confident that during your leadership in the White House, your presence as our First Lady will motivate many girls and young women around the world to follow their dreams. President-elect Obama's messages of hope and change are more than slogans. They encourage us to develop a positive mind-set about our ability and capacity to achieve.

As a health professional, I applaud the President-elect for making health care a priority in his agenda. I also encourage you to add health care as part of your focus as First Lady. In addition to the promotion of quality health care for all and the elimination of disparities, your support will inspire many women to fulfill their dreams of becoming health care professionals and providers.

Mrs. Obama, I am extremely proud of you and your family. We know that our new first family will represent the United States well. I will continue to keep you and your family in my prayers as you continue on your history-making journey. Please accept my sincere gratitude for your positive representation of women young and old, Black and white. Good luck to you and your family and may God continue to bless you. Finally and in keeping with the spirit of your campaign, I say **"Yes we can!"**

Sincerely,

Gladys Jean Diji

Gladys Jean Diji resides in Buffalo, New York. She is a nurse specializing in mental health and is a member of several service organizations. She has a long history of community involvement and has been the recipient of numerous awards and honors. Her hobbies include dancing and travel. She has three daughters: Renee, Lisa, and Tameka. Her husband is Augustine Diji.

Dear First Lady,

Your hard work, dedication, and courage contributed much to the victory of the Obama campaign for the presidency. You are already known around the globe and I believe you have set an extraordinary example for others to follow.

Having been a citizen of Washington, D.C., for many years, I have been fortunate enough to observe the planning for the last four presidential inaugurations and join in the celebrations on Inauguration Day. Each one has been very carefully planned and has been very different. For the current inauguration, I have witnessed unparalleled excitement inside and outside the D.C. area as preparations have been made to welcome the Obama family to the White House. This historic day brings unprecedented crowds, in both diversity and numbers, into this federal district. This event has challenged all local administrative and law enforcement agencies as never before while validating the message of hope that has touched so many Americans.

In observing you in the media, I am aware that you are dedicated to community service. As the President's partner and First Lady, you will be able to expand the public service to which you are so devoted and about which you are so passionate to nationwide and worldwide spheres. Also your new role will offer fresh opportunities for success. I am excited because you will bring new ideas, unique talents, and unyielding motivation to the forefront and you will be in a position to influence the lives of others more than ever before.

You will walk down a road shared only by a few dedicated individuals who have come before you while facing new challenges, new responsibilities, and new expectations. Your new role adds to all of your current roles. As you build your legacy as First Lady of the United States of America, all eyes will continue to be on you. Be ever mindful that the spirit of the American people will always be there to support you. As you face all of the new challenges you will encounter, I believe you will remain a heartening example for the American people.

Sincerely,

Betty K. Falato

Betty K. Falato resides in Washington, D.C., where she continues her research about the educational environment in Pottawatomie County, Oklahoma, where she attended primary and secondary schools.

Dear Michelle,

First let me say . . . "Congratulations!!!!" Then, let me say, "You go, girl!!!!!"

My real connection to you began when the media was "hammering you" for saying: "For the first time in my adult life, I am proud of my country."

When that statement was the sensational news of the moment, I had many thoughts, and I would like to share some of them:

—I believed it was important to remember that you grew up as a young woman of color on the South Side of Chicago. Princeton or not, I'm quite sure that you, your family, friends, had lived through a myriad of situations that could make you cry, be angry, be many things . . . the least of which was "proud." I wanted people to have realistic expectations. I was praying that you would not deny your experiences, and whatever it was in your heart, that prompted those words, your experiences were real for you, and they are to be honored and respected.

—I wished that I could tell you, don't change yourself for anyone . . . as a woman of color, going to the higher education institutions that you did and working in the profession that you did, you, like me, and countless others, have had to learn "survival skills." You have had to learn the behaviors, the speech patterns, and the nuances of the majority culture to survive and, though I absolutely do not subscribe to the "too white" point of view, I believe that there is a reality of survival. While that may be so, I desperately want you to hold on to, and visibly honor, your heritage . . . all of it! For example, I wish that when you get to the White House, if you should so choose, that you would feel free to get the meals that remind you of your childhood, as much as you want.

Throughout the campaign, as I watched you become the icon of American fashion and watched you become the model for working mothers and loving wives everywhere, fist bump and all, I felt a kinship. I am also a wife, and a working mother, with never enough time to do it all the way I wish I could. You said you want to be the best "First Mom." I'm sure it will be tough, so, it's great that your Mom will join you in the White House. Grandma's presence will be a steadying influence for Malia and Sasha.

I appreciate the interests you expressed as potential work once you become First Lady, e.g., working with those military families, so vital for our country. If you offer opportunities to volunteer, I would certainly raise a hand. As President-elect Obama says, we will all have to do our part.

Michelle, I wish you all the BEST!! You will take your place among the great First Ladies of the U.S.A., and I'll be with you in Spirit all the way!!

Althea Goodison-Orr

Althea Goodison-Orr is a resident of West Orange, New Jersey.

Dear Michelle,

My grandmother Ella was born in 1906 in South Carolina. After her parents died she and her four sisters moved to Washington, D.C., in 1916. She remembered the horrors of the Red Summer that saw the lives of so many African Americans taken by jealous and hate-filled Whites. In 1922, Ella married Whitfield, a minister, from her hometown. Their fifth child, Barbara, was born during the Great Depression in 1935. Barbara was always active in the struggle and still speaks of how she stood next to Jackie Robinson at the 1963 March on Washington. I am the fifth child of Barbara and I was born in the year that "hope" died, 1968. This was also the year that my father started a youth employment program in Washington, D.C., with Marion Barry. This organization became The Mayor's Summer Youth Employment Program.

Having the genetic predisposition to fight for what's right, I stood up against Apartheid and marched in front of the South African Embassy in the late '80s. Now, my first child, Leontyn Ella Gbegan, was born November 12th of this year. Now I tell everyone that she arrived the year that "hope" was reborn in the skin of your husband. To see you two together is so beautiful. I know my ancestors are looking at you and your family through my eyes. I am so happy that my daughter, whose father is from Benin, West Africa, will know that it is possible even for her to become President of the United States. It is incredible that her mother, who used history as proof that this country was not ready for a Black man to be in control of its future, now believes that her African and African American daughter really has no limitations.

When I was eight, I thought my Cher and Black Christie Barbie dolls were the best representations of women of color. They didn't look poor, shabby, or unacceptable by the media's standards. Now my daughter has you. Your obviously African features looking like wealth, style, and trend setting have turned me from perpetual skeptic to grand proponent of "grand hope." This is a great thing for a teacher to have. Thank you for being such a balanced, beautiful, intellectual, generous mother figure to my daughter and my students at Lindblom Math & Science Academy on the South Side of Chicago, and to children of African descent all over the world.

Turning wind into energy and energy into what matters,

Toni Asante Lightfoot

Toni Asante Lightfoot is a native of Washington, D.C., now living in exile in Chicago. There she teaches in several schools, after-school programs, and is currently the coordinator of WordsAlive!, a program that teaches teachers how to teach poetry to first through fifth graders across content areas. Lightfoot has been published in several anthologies and lent her poems and voice to several CD projects.

Dear Michelle,

November 4, 2008—Yes, we DID! Barack Obama, President-elect 2008! To put this in perspective, I was born during the Civil Rights Movement and the first man landed on the moon on my first birthday, July 20th, 1969. In my 40th year, I am blessed to be given the opportunity to witness the first African-American become the President-elect, 2008. YES WE DID!

Those who truly know me know that I began supporting Barack following the 2004 Democratic National Convention. However, a few weeks ago, on October 22, 2008, my support for him advanced to a new level when I decided to take my entire family to Obama's rally here in Richmond. With kids in tow . . . we waited outside for more than two hours, but the rally was priceless. Honestly, I can not express the memories it provided nor the inspiration it provided to my husband to finally acquire citizenship.

Beyond that experience, I involved myself in many aspects of this campaign including donating money, volunteering time to call potential voters, logging data, and preparing canvassing materials. All of this elevated my support even more. I can honestly say the VICTORY in Virginia is sweeter.

In the end I know our country still has many challenges to conquer, but we have crossed a major hurdle today. I know that I chose HOPE over FEAR to CHANGE this country and this world!! I know that I would stand in line another two hours to see Obama, or another forty-five minutes to cast my vote for this sort of historic result: A NEW AMERICA for my children. Truly, I know many have awaited this moment longer than I and I wish I could share it with my grandmother. She, like Barack's grandmother, instilled the urgency and importance of a good education.

With that knowledge I have come to know that as an educator, as a woman, and most importantly as a parent, the possibility of making the IMPOSSIBLE POSSIBLE restores my faith in the belief: IMPOSSIBLE IS NOTHING! It restores my faith in knowing that "Rosa sat so Martin could walk . . . Martin walked so Obama could run . . . Obama ran so children of the future can FLY to new heights!"

A. Katrise Perera

A. Katrise Perera's Creole roots began in the bayous of Louisiana, but she currently calls Richmond, Virginia, her home, where she lives with her husband of seventeen years and their twin twelve-year-old daughters.

Dear Mrs. Obama,

Congratulations for the victory that you share with your spouse, President-Elect Barack Hussein Obama. As you are well aware, your victory is shared throughout the world. I witnessed this victory in Buea, Cameroon, West Africa where I was attending the first conference of the International Conference on African and Caribbean Literature (ICACL) with faculty and students from Morehouse College. As we entered the nation, the customs agent asked if we had voted before we came because we would have to go back to vote if we had not. I was proud to tell him that I had voted affirmatively for Barack Obama in the early voting procedure. That sentiment was echoed by many persons in Cameroon.

On election night the people of Buea watched, waited, and celebrated with us at the hotel. The announcement of Obama's victory came at the poetic moment of day's dawn in Buea. The sunrise was bold, fire-red and full and sat majestically at the top of Mount Buea, one of the tallest mountains in Africa. We rejoiced with our African sisters and brothers.

I began to pull from my African American memory the songs and poetry that I held onto during my lifetime as a black female in America. We held hands in a circle and sang proudly, *Lift Every Voice and Sing* from the *Negro National Anthem* by James Weldon Johnson, both at the hotel and later at the closing ceremonies at the University of Buea. But, in my private moments, I kept mumbling the stanzas from a poem that I learned as a little girl when I first discovered that I loved literature. That poem is *For My People* by Margaret Walker:

For my people standing staring trying to fashion a better way
from confusion, from hypocrisy and misunderstanding,
trying to fashion a world that will hold all the people,
all the faces, all the adams and eves and their countless
generations;

Let a new earth rise. Let another world be born. Let a

bloody peace be written in the sky. Let a second
generation full of courage issue forth; let a people
loving freedom come to growth. Let a beauty full of
healing and a strength of final clenching be the pulsing
in our spirits and our blood. Let the martial songs be
written, let the dirges disappear. Let a race of men now
rise and take control.

It is so poignant that we have been reciting this poem for over half a century and here you come as an answer to the hope of generations that is encapsulated in the poem.

I saw you and Barack Obama coming like a meteor blazing a trail across the sky, "bright before us like the morning sun"! I incorporated his autobiography, *Dreams From My Father*, into the coursework of all of my *Research Writing* courses over the past four years to demonstrate to my college students, who are predominantly African American males, how to research their family history. The lessons that they learned were greater than that. They learned the importance of understanding their relationships to their fathers no matter how tenuous. They learned the imperative of reconstructing their family narrative into the larger context of an American narrative and ultimately into the annals of global history. Through your story, a cadre of students emerged with composition skills and their identities in tact.

I am so grateful to you and your husband for preparing yourself for excellence and leadership in such a way that you could bring forth the fruition of our dreams and the hopes of the whole world. As a mother, also, of two daughters I applaud your devotion to them and the priority of rearing them in the way they should go. You have all of my prayers and best wishes and anything that I might offer.

Leah Creque

Leah Creque is an Assistant Professor of English at Morehouse College in Atlanta, Georgia. She received her undergraduate degree from Wellesley College, her master's degree from Atlanta University and her doctorate from Emory University. Currently, she is working on several publications in her research interests of African dance and Caribbean literature. She has two grown daughters, Kyla and Reva. She spends time trying to improve her game of bridge, taking long walks at Stone Mountain Park and indulging the family cat, Tabasco

Dear First Lady Michelle,

My name is Tammie Hill. I was born in Oklahoma City, Oklahoma. In 1994 I became Mayor of Lima, Oklahoma. This tiny town is one of the original all-Black Towns of Oklahoma. A lot has changed since it was first founded by African Americans in the last 1800's. White settlers came in 1926 when the Greater Seminole Oil Field was discovered. Today there is only a handful of people in this historic town.

The Census of 2000 reported that there were 74 people, 30 households, and 18 families residing in the town. It is quite a bit less since 2000 because a number of our older people have passed away. None of the young people stay in the town anymore. There is no work for them here. In 2000, the racial makeup of the town was 43.24% white, 36.49% African American, 5.41% Native American, and 14.86% from two or more other ethnic groups. Latinos make up 2.70% of the population. The racial makeup of the town has not changed much. Since 2000,the median income for a household in the town was $18,750, and the median income for a family was $15,625. That's not a lot of money and there is unequal pay between men and women. Even in Lima, males still made more than females with a median income of $23,125 for males versus $14,375 for females.

People in Lima don't have very much disposable income. In 2000 47.4% of families and 59.7% of the population lived below the poverty line, including 70.4% of those young people under 18 and 40.0% of those over 64. Little has changed since 2000. However, while it may look like nothing much is happening here in Lima, we still have something to celebrate; its Lima's Rosenwall Hall School. In addition, I also have you and Barack to celebrate. You can't imagine how pleased I am.

As you can see from the census statistics, the town has only a few people who make just a little bit of money—But, Lima is a special place for us with its extraordinary history. Lima is recognized in the State as a historic town that was incorporated on April 8, 1913. We especially take pride in the fact that Lima is one of the original all-Black Towns in Oklahoma.

I know that all of those Black folks, who stepped out on faith to build those early Black towns against terrible odds, are walking around God's heaven and tipping their hats to you and Barack. It must be a sight to see. Even though we are small and getting smaller, we like to celebrate good things here in Lima. In 1995, working with the townspeople, we managed to get April 8 proclaimed as Lima, Oklahoma Day. We call it Limafest Day and it is a day of fun and recreation with games, fashion shows, commercial vendors selling their products and basketball tournaments. It is my greatest hope to see that the town of Lima, Oklahoma establishes a park, a fire department, a shopping mall, a technology center for seniors and youths to become computer literate, a crisis center for youth and adults to receive counseling and to become more productive in society. We haven't been able to achieve these goals because of numerous obstacles but we are still working on it, and we have some things we are proud of.

We are especially proud of our historic school, Rosenwald Hall. I don't know if you know this but Rosenwald Hall was built with the philanthropy of Julius Rosenwald of Sears and Roebuck. Rosenwald helped to build more than 5300 schools for Black children all across the South and Southwest. He provided matching grant money. In order to match the Rosenwald contribution, Black women really did their part. They baked pies, planted gardens and sold produce from their home gardens, made quilts and worked in other ways to contribute to the building of Lima's first school for Black children. Sasha and Malia will attend Sidwell, a private school in Washington D.C., but I sure wish they could see and understand something about Rosenwald, the first school for Black children in Lima, Oklahoma. Rosenwald's heyday is over and the school is in disrepair and run down. It's kind of hard to get the townspeople to pay any attention to preserving Rosenwald Hall. A few years ago some people in the town decided to move and create another town just down the street. They call it New Lima. I am working to make sure that the old Lima doesn't just fade away and that the extraordinary history of this historically all-Black Town does not disappear. The old Lima with historic Rosenwald Hall is still a bright spot for the residents. But for me, a new bright spot in the history of this country is that you, Michelle, one of our own Sistahs is going to the White House to be the First Lady for the entire country and you are taking your children and your mother with you. I could not be more proud.

On January 20, 2009, you and your family will be in Washington, D.C., in front of the largest Inaugural crowd ever for a President of the United States. I can hardly imagine the size of that crowd and the crush of humanity that will be there to see Barack and you, Michelle, first African American man and his African American wife to take the oath for the highest office in the land. I can't come to be with all those others who will be there to see you but I am sending you joy and love from me, my children, Marcus Garvey, Christian Earl and Ashley

Janay and the little town of Lima. We wish you the best in your new job in Washington, D.C. After you get settled into your new house I hope you and your girls can take a trip to Lima and celebrate with us on Limafest Day and you can see the Rosenwald Hall that we are trying to preserve. We would love to have you and we will leave the lights on for you!

Again, we have you in our thoughts and prayers and wish you and President-elect Obama the best of everything. So just stay true to yourself, keep God with you and take care of yourself and your family.

Sincerely,

Tammie Hill

Tammie Hill is the Mayor of the historically Black Oklahoma Town of Lima. She is also a member of the Association of Black Mayors.

THE OBAMA LESSON . . . A FAMILY PRAYER

Please join us as we thank *Spirit*
for each and every blessing & miracle
that has manifested in our lives,
and the lives of all others throughout the Universe.

It is time to end ALL violence,
for forgiveness,
and a massive healing
so that we begin to accept
that separation of any kind
moves us away from our *Collective Self.*

WE ARE ONE
in mind, body & spirit.
We each have a responsibility
to open our hearts,
and to learn to love unconditionally.

If asked how does one fight assimilation???
then we must consider this response—
we don't . . .
because the idea is to grow in LOVE.

We merge with Divine Consciousness.
This is our Spiritual Journey.
This is the reason why
we are here on Mother Earth=Heart.

For some of us, then the question becomes,
"How do I maintain my identity?"
The only true identity that we have
is to be *ONE In Spirit*

That is not to say
that we should ignore
our individual birth cultures.
On the contrary . . .
part of our journey to Spirit
is to have an understanding
of the many paths that we,
and our hopeful ancestors have taken.

With hope we can continue to learn to see more clearly,
and to work to live with understanding,
compassion, and a strong sense of self,
which is *OUR her* and *his story.*

Please join us in affirmation . . .
Today I pray for strength,
courage, and hope.

I release my fear.

I speak the truth.

I honor my hopeful ancestors.

I nurture my children and my entire family.

I believe in economic empowerment.

I walk as a leader,
a diplomat & a visionary.

I look at my brothers & sisters,
some lost,
and open my arms to show the way.

Together we stand
in the reflection pool
of our ancestors,
and join them in hope
and celebration of the
ongoing journey to re-membering LOVE . . .

And So It Is With Love,

Rev. Melony McGant

Melony McGant, aka Miss Mellie Rainbow, is the daughter of Betty J. Tilman. She is a marketing director for a productions company. She is also a storyteller and interfaith minister passionate about children learning, sharing with hope, healing and love.

HOLD YOUR HEAD UP HIGH.
WE ARE GOING WITH YOU.

Dear Michelle,

It is said that those who achieve greatness are the result of those who have struggled before them.

When you move into the White House as this Nation's first African-American First Lady, you will not be alone. The women that were captured in Africa and brought to this country to become women of bondage are going with you. Their struggle to live a life that would never be their own again, with no end in sight, was their only will to live. But they somehow knew that this day would come. These women, who toiled in the rice and cotton fields and lost children because of their back-breaking labor or gave birth only to have these children taken and sold away from them anyway . . . are going with you.

HOLD YOUR HEAD UP HIGH.
WE ARE GOING WITH YOU.

The women in this country who struggled to feed their families during the Great Depression, like my great-grandmother, are going with you. She buried her husband and eight-day-old infant on the same day. Her struggle to raise four children by herself and take care of her mother forced her to wash other people's clothes for a living; a living that barely provided a biscuit and a little bit of coffee for her children to eat as they went off to school. This was a time that was characterized by extreme violence against people of color in the South. Despair was all around her.

HOLD YOUR HEAD UP HIGH.
WE ARE GOING WITH YOU.

Women like my grandmother, who, with only an eighth-grade education, toiled everyday cleaning other people's houses. She was the sole breadwinner of a family with an alcoholic husband, an aging mother and one small little girl. She left the South during the Great Migration in search of a better life and opportunity, only to find a life of heartache and back-breaking work. Her faith in God was what sustained her and her family until her death on Nov. 5, 2008. Just two and a half hours after your husband gave his historic victory speech.

HOLD YOUR HEAD UP HIGH.
WE ARE GOING WITH YOU.

Women like my mother, a single Mom, who has worked tirelessly to provide for her family. She worked two jobs, seven days a week for over a decade to provide for me and my grandmother. She enabled me to go to one of this country's best Conservatory's of Music so I could follow my dream of becoming a musician, marry and become a mother myself, all the while battling breast cancer and caring for her aging mother. Now that her mother is gone she can finally live the life she put off for almost 60 years.

HOLD YOUR HEAD UP HIGH.
WE ARE GOING WITH YOU.

These are the women who have sustained this country through its darkest hours. Their stories can be found in any family. These are the women who are going to the White House with you. Their strength will give you your strength.

So, Michelle . . . HOLD YOUR HEAD UP HIGH.
WE ARE GOING WITH YOU.

Janeen Ceparano Wilkins

Janeen Ceparano Wilkins is a resident of Rochester, New York, where she is a performing violist. She is the recipient of several notable awards for her musical accomplishments.